# THE
# PROFITABLE
# BUSINESS
# AUTHOR

Library and Archives Canada Cataloguing in Publication

Eason, Julie Anne, 1968-, author
    The profitable business author : how to write a book that attracts clients and customers / Julie Anne Eason.

ISBN 978-1-77141-143-1 (paperback)

1. Self-publishing.  I. Title.

Z285.5.E28 2015          070.5          C2015-905839-2

# THE PROFITABLE BUSINESS AUTHOR

## How to Write a Book That Attracts Clients and Customers

JULIE ANNE EASON

Copyright © 2015 by Julie Anne Eason

All rights reserved. No part of this publication may be reproduced, stored in or introduced into a retrieval system, or transmitted, in any form, or by any means (electronic, mechanical, photocopying, recording or otherwise) without the prior written permission of the publisher. This book is sold subject to the condition that it shall not, by way of trade or otherwise, be lent, resold, hired out, or otherwise circulated without the publisher's prior consent in any form of binding or cover other than that in which it is published and without a similar condition including this condition being imposed on the subsequent purchaser.

Book Cover Design: Miladinka Milic
Portrait Photographer: Joel Tsui
Typeset: Greg Salisbury

DISCLAIMER: This is a work of non-fiction. The information is of a general nature to help you on the subject of business writing. Readers of this publication agree that Julie Anne Eason will not be held responsible or liable for damages that may be alleged or resulting directly or indirectly from their use of this publication. All external links are provided as a resource only and are not guaranteed to remain active for any length of time. The author cannot be held accountable for the information provided by, or actions resulting from accessing these resources.

# DEDICATION

For my husband, James
Thank you for always believing in me.
The best is yet to come.

# BONUS: Download the Companion Workbook

Want to get a head start on your book?

Download the PDF companion workbook for this edition right now, and work along as you read.

1: Go to TheProfitableBusinessAuthor.com

2. Click on "Companion Workbook"

3. Tell us where to email the access link

The workbook helps you work on your book while you're reading this book.

# CONTENTS

**Foreword** ........................................................................... XI
By Russell Brunson

**How Can a Book Build Your Business?** ................................. 1
    Can every business use this strategy? ................................. 6
    Why are books so powerful, anyway? .................................. 8
    But what if . . . ? ................................................................... 9
    The six stages of creating a book ........................................ 11

**Planning** ............................................................................ 17
    What's the overall goal (or goals) for your book? ................ 19
    Who is your target reader? .................................................. 20
    How to read your readers' minds ........................................ 21
    Are you writing the right book for your business? .............. 23
    Preliminary title .................................................................. 28
    Start thinking about a cover now ....................................... 31
    How to get endorsements ................................................... 32
    How to pre-sell readers on your expertise .......................... 33
    Plan out your budget ......................................................... 36

**Writing** .............................................................................. 41
    The secret to a great outline .............................................. 44
    How do you build a framework? ......................................... 52
    19 Nonfiction book elements to consider including in your book ........... 53
    Different ways to write a book ............................................ 60
    Finding your unique voice .................................................. 69
    Images and artwork ............................................................ 70

>    Front and back matter ................................................................. 71
>    Time management ...................................................................... 73

## Editing ............................................................................................... 81
>    What should you edit at this stage? ........................................... 84
>    When to hire a professional editor ............................................ 85
>    Beta readers .................................................................................. 88
>    How to hire an editor .................................................................. 93
>    How much do editors charge and how long does it take? ...... 96
>    How to help your editor .............................................................. 97

## Publishing and Distribution ........................................................ 103
>    What exactly does a publisher do? ........................................... 105
>    Here's the dirty little secret about publishing ....................... 108
>    The pros and cons of different publishing models ............... 109
>       Traditional publishing .......................................................... 110
>       Independent (indie) publishing .......................................... 112
>       Self-publishing ...................................................................... 113
>       Hybrid publishing ................................................................. 115
>    Distribution basics .................................................................... 116
>    Bookstore distribution .............................................................. 117
>    Online retailers .......................................................................... 120
>    Bypass distribution and special sales ...................................... 122

## Marketing ...................................................................................... 129
>    Book marketing basics .............................................................. 130
>       Website .................................................................................... 131
>       Email marketing .................................................................... 134
>       Social media marketing ........................................................ 135
>       Online marketing .................................................................. 137

    Offline marketing ........................................................................... 139
    Which method works best? ............................................................ 140
    What is a platform and how do you build one? ........................... 142
    How to borrow other people's platforms ..................................... 143
    How to encourage word of mouth ................................................ 145
    Should you give away your book? ................................................. 152
    Getting reviews ............................................................................... 153
    Throw a party! ................................................................................ 154

**Profiting From Your Book** ............................................................... 159
    How do you really make money with a book? ............................ 160
    Types of back end products ........................................................... 161
    Types of back end services ............................................................. 162
    Organize your back end into a logical progression ..................... 164
    How to move people through your product progression ........... 165

**Conclusion**   171
    What to expect as you write your book ........................................ 171
Procrasti-what? ..................................................................................... 173
    Immediate action steps .................................................................. 178

**You're Invited** ..................................................................................... 181

# FOREWORD

Ten years ago, I had the idea that I wanted to write a book. I had seen the power of books as tools for building and growing a company and knew it would help me reach my goals faster. So, that first day I told myself *I want my own book*, I sat down and started to write it.

About fifteen minutes into writing, I realized why most people don't actually write books. It was really hard. I knew what I wanted to say. It was all in my head, but getting it out of my head and into a book was a lot harder than I thought it would be. At that time, I decided to pause and just step away from the project.

A few months later, I came back to it and tried to move forward again. I immediately ran into a big stumbling block. I don't know what it was that stopped me, but I just couldn't move forward. I stepped back, took a break, and then tried again a few months later.

This process continued on and off for over ten years!

I remember watching some of my peers and colleagues at the time. I felt that we were at the same level. But for some reason, other people perceived my colleagues as more accomplished and further along in their businesses. I discovered that this perception existed not because they were more accomplished, but simply because they had written books. They were authors. And that was something special.

I remember one night a friend and I were at dinner talking about business and growth strategy and things we were going to do.

My friend said, "You know what? It's amazing to me that you

still haven't written a book after all these years. You've seen what's happened to author A and author B and author C, these people who are our peers. You've seen what's happened to their companies because of their books. As successful as you are, I'm amazed you've never finished."

I remember sitting there, frustrated at myself for not writing a book sooner, and upset that the process was so much harder than I thought it was going to be. I had so much fear and anxiety tied around it. My stomach was actually in knots at the thought of this project. It's not like I hadn't been writing my whole life. My business depended on me writing sales pages, advertising, emails, and all sorts of things. What was the big deal about a book?

That night I thought, *You know what? I have to do this. I can't wait any longer.* And I realized I wasn't going to be able to do it myself. So I went online and started searching for somebody to help me. Luckily, within about two days of searching and interviewing people, I had a chance to meet Julie. Despite my fears of moving forward on this project, I also had enough pain at this point that I knew it had to happen.

After spending a couple hours on the phone with Julie, I knew that she was the person who was going to help me get there. She understood my goals for the book. She knew my target audience. And she helped me feel confident that *this time* we could finally make it to the finish line.

We first started planning the chapter structures and figuring out the right flow. From there, we built out the sections, the content, and the information. Then we spent some time creating an audio recording of each chapter. I tried to write them and just couldn't get it out, so I recorded each chapter instead. Eventually, we put on a whole three-day live event so that I could speak the chapters. I felt much more comfortable speaking, so we did that. Julie led me through the writing, editing, and publishing. We went through this whole process to create the book together.

I have to tell you that the entire process from beginning to end was not simple, which is probably why more people don't write books.

But the end result was amazing!

When the book was finished, I felt an unbelievable sense of accomplishment. I still remember getting the first copy and holding it in my hands. The cover just felt different. Something about it felt so exciting. I flipped through the pages and saw the words. I saw what had been bottled up in my head for ten years, finally in a format where anybody could look at it, read it, touch it, experience it, and get results from it. It was amazing!

I got so excited when we decided to launch this and start selling the book. We coordinated a great product launch around it. In the first thirty days, we sold 25,000 copies of the book. I wasn't just an author. I was a best-selling author!

Now you may be wondering, "Russell, what happened on the back side of that?"

The answer is I don't know the full impact yet. A lot of good things have already started to happen, for sure. But this book is so evergreen it will continue to serve me this year, next year, and 10 years from now. What did the book do for me? I don't know what heights are even possible yet. It will definitely be a part of everything else we do moving forward.

I can tell you what's happened so far, though. A week after we launched the book, one of our readers received a copy. I don't even know how he found it, but he read the book and was so excited that he called our office. Two days later, he wrote me a check for $100,000 to come out to train his team on the principles inside the book.

The book has been responsible for dozens of people joining our Inner Circle coaching and high-end mastermind groups. It has also helped us push our software company forward. The book trains people on the correct way to use our software to grow their companies. It's helped us exponentially grow our company, and not just through lead generation. We now have a single document that codifies everything we teach and do for our clients.

When people come to us, they already have a basic understanding of why we can get such great results for them. They come to us practically pre-sold. And we get to help people who may never be able to work with us directly. An individual can only help so many people with consulting or products; with a book, that person can help millions.

For those of you who might be wondering if you should write a book . . .
For those of you who've tried and are wondering if it's worth the effort . . .
For those of you who have any kind of fear or worry that's holding you back from jumping in and just doing it . . .

I want to tell you that Julie is the person who helped me. Without her, it never would have come out of my head. I would have been stuck for maybe another decade or more. But now my book has the chance to bless and to serve tens of thousands of people's lives around the world. And thanks to the skillful construction of the content, it will continue to do that for the next ten or twenty years—or even longer.

I also want to tell you that you don't have to go it alone. In fact, *don't do it alone*. There are so many variables and roadblocks you just don't even realize are there until they stop you dead in your tracks. You need someone experienced to offer you the support and guidance to quickly bypass those roadblocks and get on with the writing.

Your book is important. There are people who need to read it. The longer it stays in your head, the longer those people have to wait. Get help! Use this book as a guide to help you through the process. It works. I'm living proof.

Thank you, Julie, for your help, your guidance, and your ability to get these words out of my head and into a format that can help change other people's lives.

Russell Brunson

Best-selling author of *DotComSecrets: The Underground Playbook for Growing Your Company Online*

# CHAPTER ONE

# HOW CAN A BOOK BUILD YOUR BUSINESS?

Imagine you're looking for help. You need a company that can solve a huge problem quickly, a company that's trustworthy and really knows what they're doing. You don't have time to mess around with amateurs.

So you browse through a few companies online. Their websites look good, but how can you really tell if they can handle your problem? How do you know if you can trust them? Oh wait, one of them has a book! A book that answers your questions and demonstrates that they have real experience solving exactly the problem you're struggling with.

Which company will you choose?

If you're like millions and millions of other people around the world, you'll choose the company with the book.

I think almost everyone believes they have a book inside them, including business people. They have big messages to share. They want to have a lasting impact on the world. They want to expand their reach beyond what basic advertising can offer.

Sound familiar?

They may flirt with the idea of calling themselves authors. Maybe they picture themselves sipping wine with the literati at an outdoor café in the shadow of the Eiffel Tower. Sometimes they may feel like it's a romantic notion that could never really happen.

Except it can.

Speakers, coaches, experts, service providers, CEOs and entrepreneurs—business people of all sorts are discovering that becoming an author isn't just a far-off pipe dream. It's possible. And it's a powerful strategic advantage in their businesses.

In the not-so-distant past, a handful of large publishing houses controlled the literary scene. Agents and acquisition editors decided which lucky few writers would be granted the gift of publication. If you wanted to be published, you had to jump through all sorts of bureaucratic hoops. And if you were lucky, you might see your book in print. Or, if you were really tenacious, you might pay out your life savings to a vanity publisher. They would print and ship you huge boxes of books, which most likely spent the rest of their days in your garage.

That was then, and this is now.

With advances in electronic and print-on-demand publishing, as well as overall access to marketing channels, just about anyone can become an author these days. Whether you choose to figure it all out on your own, or you hire independent contractors to help, writing and publishing your own book is completely within your reach. Here's what I believe: Your business should have a book. And your book should build your business.

So, how exactly can a book build your business? Let's take a look.

## A Book Can Position You as an Expert.

If you weren't an expert on a topic, you probably wouldn't be writing a book about it. And let's face it—if you're in business, you are an expert. Becoming an author validates that expert status and proclaims it to the world. You don't have to be the highest authority on your subject. An expert is just someone who knows more than the average Joe. So, if you've been in business for two years, maybe you don't know more than someone who's been around for 20 years. But you're still an expert compared to total beginners. There will always be someone who knows more than you. That doesn't change the fact that you know plenty, and you can share that knowledge in a book.

## A Book Can Drive Traffic to Your Website or Store.

Your website is useless if no one visits it. The same can be said for your bricks-and-mortar store. It really doesn't matter how amazing your products or services are. If no one sees them, they'll just sit on the shelves gathering dust. Traffic generation is critical to the success of your business. And "traffic" is just people. Naturally, people want to do business with an expert. So, if your book does its job and educates people about your company, they will naturally wind up on your website or on your doorstep. By the time you've finished reading this book, you'll know exactly what you need to write to show them the way.

## A Book Can Open Doors to New Opportunities.

Ever thought about being paid to speak? Do you think your service could help larger groups of people, if only you had access to them? Wish you could get through the gatekeepers and gain access to that bigwig client? With a book, you can often bypass gatekeepers and bureaucratic red tape. You'll be surprised how the doors to golden opportunities can magically swing wide open when you are an author. People will want to interview you. Clients will seek you out, instead of you having to pursue them. At first, you might think it's just a weird coincidence, but no—it's your book!

## A Book Can Pre-Sell Your Products and Services.

Depending on your business, a book can actually provide many of the same functions as a full-time salesperson. Your book is always ready to explain your products and services to interested prospects. If you include the right content, your book can answer all sorts of questions for readers and actually convince them to buy the product. Then, all that's left for your sales department to do is make the close and write up the order.

By the way, you don't have to be a business *owner* to write a lead-generating book. If you're a salesperson working for someone else, it might make sense to write your own book and bring people to *your* door instead of to a competitor or another salesperson at your company.

## A Book Can Introduce Your Business to People Who Normally Wouldn't Find You.

Traditional advertising methods can only get you so far. Even if you have a huge budget, and you cover all the bases with online, offline, and pay-per-click ads, there will always be pockets of people who never see your ads. You can't be everywhere all the time. When you're an author, you're visible in one of the largest search engines in the world. No, not Google—Amazon! People search Amazon.com every day looking to purchase all sorts of things. Remember, Amazon started out selling books. And today they are the largest seller of print and electronic books in the world. Claiming your spot in that search engine gives you exposure to potentially millions of new clients and customers—people who might never find you otherwise.

## A Book Gives You Something Tangible to Give Prospects.

Business cards are *so* 1990s. What happens to all the billions of business cards that change hands every year? Most of them wind up in the trash, long forgotten. Why? Because they don't provide value to the receiver. However, a book is a valuable item. We're taught from childhood to revere and value books. When was the last time you just tossed a book into the trash? Most people will at least skim books before passing them on to someone else, or filing the books for future reference on their shelves.

When you give someone a book instead of a card, you stand out. People remember you.

(And you can always attach your business card to the book, if you need to get rid of your stash.)

Another way to distribute something tangible to prospects is to add your book to gift bags at conventions, seminars, and conferences. Many businesses will give away items such as branded pens, notebooks, chocolate bars, or maybe postcards with discount codes on them. These items are easy to ignore. But when attendees see an actual book in their gift bags, they take notice. And if your book is truly useful and full of value, many recipients will actually seek you out during the event. When was the last time you received a postcard or pen and went looking for the company that donated it?

## Can Every Business Use This Strategy?

Absolutely! It doesn't matter if your business is B2B, B2C, online, local bricks-and-mortar, service-based, consulting, a small start-up, or a multi-national conglomerate—every business can benefit from a book.

When I do interviews, I often challenge the host to stump me: Name any business, and I can come up with a book that will give it added exposure in the marketplace and help it grow. It's a fun game, and I've never been beaten! Here are a few examples:

- A B2B accountant might write a book on how certain businesses can save on their taxes.

- A B2C toy company might write a parenting guide about educational games for preschoolers.
- A freelance writer might write a book about how businesses can improve their content marketing.
- A local dry cleaner might write a fabric care guide.
- A local restaurant might write a tourist guide about the local culture, or a recipe book.
- An e-commerce kitchen business might write a comparison guide for different makes and models of appliances.
- A global machine manufacturer might write a repair guide or a book that details how they offer a better value than their competitor(s).
- A network marketer might write two books: one about the business opportunity and one about the product.

The reason a book works for any business is because every business revolves around people. Every business needs to attract prospects and convert them into clients or customers. A book does some of that talking for you. It's part of a conversation. Many would-be authors I talk to can't figure out what to write because they're looking in the wrong place. They're looking inside themselves.

Your prospects and customers will tell you exactly what to write. All you have to do is listen! If you follow the book planning and writing strategies I have laid out in the upcoming chapters, you will start by identifying your target audience, figuring out what they want to know, and then writing the book *they* would want to read.

Now, it's important to realize that not every book is going

to be the kind of thing you'll find at Barnes & Noble. In fact, you might not even sell your book at all. You might give it away to customers or prospects. That doesn't make you any less an author, or the book any less beneficial. After all, we're not talking about *Harry Potter* here. We're talking about business books that serve a particular purpose.

## Why Are Books So Powerful, Anyway?

Have you ever wondered why authors are so special? What's the big deal about writing a book? Why do we consider it some Herculean feat?

I believe it's because the first really important "big person" job we're given as children is learning how to read. And whether you succeeded at that task or struggled with it, you knew books were important. Your parents, your teachers, all the major authority figures in your life stressed the importance of reading books at some point. Maybe you had a favorite bedtime story. Maybe you enjoyed curling up with Dr. Seuss or J.K. Rowling. Or maybe you were a *Goosebumps* kid. It makes sense that somewhere deep down we have a reverence for the written word.

Now, think forward a little to your high school and college years. Did you dread writing papers? Even if you loved to read, did you love to write? Whether you got As on every paper or they all came back covered in red marks, writing was a task.

A graded assignment.

Something that was *judged*.

We learned in school that writing is *hard*.

When you look at it this way, it makes sense that many of us feel like writing is a burden. It's a big deal. If you struggled to write a twenty-page paper in college, how in the world are you going to write a two-hundred-page book?

Not everyone is cut out to write for a living. But if you desire to write a book to build your business, you can learn the strategies we ghostwriters use to write books fast. If you're not confident with spelling, grammar, and book construction, that's what editors are for. Even if you hate to write, suck it up for a little while and your business will reap the benefits for years to come. The reverence for books that makes you a little nervous about writing your own is the same force that makes your prospects perceive you differently once you're an author.

## But What If . . .

Right now you're probably either excited to get moving forward or you're still a little nervous and hesitant. Rest assured, if you're not at least a little nervous now, you will be at some point. The doubts and negative self-talk will crop up at some point in the process. I've never met an author who didn't say, "You know, when I was writing this book, I thought I must be crazy. Who would ever want to read a book I wrote?"

It's important that you understand *it is completely normal to feel this way.*

Doubt is a human condition. It means you care about what you're writing.

The doubts and negative self-talk might show up in a variety of ways, including:

- Who am I to write a book?
- Who am I to call myself an expert?

- Who's going to listen to me?
- What if no one buys it?
- What if I get bad reviews?
- But I failed English, what if it's really no good?
- But I hate to write, how am I going to get this done?
- But I'm so busy! Where am I going to find the time?
- Blah, blah, blah . . .

No one is immune. We all feel this way sometimes. When you start hearing the What-Ifs, take a step back and realize it's just your subconscious trying to keep you safe. To keep you right where you are. To keep you from moving forward. Why? Because writing a book and putting it out there for people to read is risky! And, subconsciously, risk makes most of us nervous.

Don't let the What-Ifs stop you!

For every book ever published, there are thousands (maybe tens of thousands) that were started and never finished. The What-Ifs won and the writers gave up. Keep moving forward. Even if you think your writing is complete schlock. Keep moving forward. You can evaluate it later. Just keep writing. The hardest part of a book is writing the first draft. Just getting your ideas out of your head and onto the paper.

I strongly recommend you pick up a copy of Steven Pressfield's masterpiece *The War of Art*. It's a short book about resistance and procrastination, and how to overcome them. Buy it. Read it. Live it. The principles in that book will change your life, and help you get your book finished.

Chapter One

## The Six Stages of Creating a Book

Many people think authors just sit down, write out a manuscript, send it to a publisher, and they're done. If only that were true! The process is a little more complex than that. I break it down into six stages for business-building books. (Don't worry, we'll go into all six stages in detail in the upcoming chapters.)

**1. The Planning Stage:** This is where you'll make some major decisions about your book, such as who you're writing it for, what you want them to do when they're finished reading it, and how you'll convert them from reader to customer. This is the most important part of the writing process for business books. If you spend some quality time on your planning, the rest of the book will come together much more easily. Even if you've already started your book and you think you have it all planned out, I urge you to read through the planning chapter and really think about how it applies to your particular book.

**2. The Writing Stage:** At this point you will be in full-on creative mode. You build an outline that meets your goals, and write out the full draft of your book. You'll be tempted to stop. You'll tell yourself you don't have time. You'll wonder if it's worth all the effort. Just. Keep. Writing.

If you follow the system I've outlined in chapter three, you'll find that the writing is a lot easier than you might have thought. The thing to remember is: writing is just one small part of creating a book. Editing is really where the magic happens anyway, so just get through the initial writing as quickly as you can. Get the words out.

**3. The Editing Stage:** After you let the finished draft sit in a dark drawer to marinate and settle for a couple of weeks, it's time to start editing. Make no mistake—your draft will be a mess. You'll likely want to cry at how bad some parts of it appear. You may be tempted to trash the whole thing.

Take a deep breath.

This is normal.

Your draft is supposed to be a mess.

The magic is in the rewriting.

This stage can go very quickly, or it can be a laborious process that takes months or even years for some authors. One trick to making it through editing without losing your mind is to prepare thoroughly in the planning stage. The better you plan, the better your draft will be. And the better the draft, the easier the editing.

Another trick for less painful editing is to hire a professional writing coach or structural editor to help you. A second set of objective eyes on your manuscript is a really good thing.

**4. The Publishing and Distribution Stage:** Here it's time to get on with the actual publishing of your book. Whether you land a traditional publisher, go through an indie house, or self-publish, the same things need to happen. You'll finalize your cover design. You'll have the interior of the book designed and formatted. You'll request an ISBN (International Standard Book Number) and a bar code. And you'll have the book printed. You will have the opportunity to proofread a copy of the book before everything is finalized. Once your book is print-ready, you'll distribute it through bookstores, online retailers, and other outlets.

**5. The Marketing Stage:** Now the real work will begin: the marketing. This stage never really ends, unless you decide to discontinue the book. Sales is a numbers game. The more momentum you have, the easier it is to sell a lot of books. Even though I've put the marketing stage toward the end, realize that you can start building a following and marketing your book very early in the process. In fact, it's never too early to start marketing.

**6. The Profiting Stage:** While it's nice to be a best-selling author and make some money on book sales, remember that's not the ultimate goal here. Your profits will come on the back end with the sales of your products and services. You just need to make sure there's a pathway in place for your prospects to become customers. The book is a valuable introduction to you, your company, and your ability to help people. But it's not the big money maker. In fact, you might wind up giving away the majority of your books for free. Again, if you take the planning stage seriously, the profit stage will be easier, too.

## So how long does it take to get the finished product?

There are lots of experts on the Internet trying to convince you that you can have a book written, published, and sold within a weekend. As if all you have to do is copy and paste some transcriptions, upload them to Amazon, add some great sales copy, and BAM! You're a published author.

Ok. Yes. You *can* do it this way. But why would you want to? You're not going to have a high-quality representation of your business that way. Instead, you will have an embarrassment that your competitors can point to and laugh at while they're serving *your* customers!

So, let's agree right now that it's okay to take some time to get this right. Not a lot of time. But *at least* six months to a year, if you're doing the work yourself. If you're hiring a top-quality ghostwriter, and paying a company to take care of the editing, design, layout, publishing, distribution, and marketing, it could happen faster. If you choose to go this route, be prepared to pay for the convenience.

We're going for quality here. Don't rush the process.

Once you're finished, you'll have an evergreen sales tool that will naturally attract clients, customers, speaking gigs and all sorts of opportunities year in and year out.

This is a long-term game.

So, take your time and reap the rewards.

Are you ready to get started? The next chapter is all about planning for success.

Chapter One

# CASE STUDY

**Stick This!**
**Using Promotional Stickers To Build Identity, Create Word Of Mouth and Grow Sales**
By Jeff Nicholson

**Author's business:** Websticker.com (Sticker printing and marketing consulting)
**Target market:** Business owners, marketing professionals, and sticker enthusiasts

**Tell us about your book.**
The book discusses small business marketing—specifically, low-cost, high-impact, guerrilla marketing using stickers. My ultimate goal was to raise awareness of this often overlooked marketing tool and to raise my stature as the expert in the sticker industry.

**How did you find the writing process?**
It was not easy to write. I dedicated some time each morning for well over a year to get it done. I drew on past blog posts I had written and case studies from a few key clients to make the writing easier.

**Did the book help you achieve your goal?**
It's still early in the process, but I would say it is already achieving the desired goals and helping our business. The book is essential as we re-brand parts of our business and try to establish ourselves more as a sticker design and marketing

company, as opposed to a sticker printer (which is now a crowded, commodity-based industry).

## Chapter Two

## Planning

*The good news is that*
*just about anyone can become an author these days.*

*The bad news is that*
*just about anyone can become an author these days!*

There's a LOT of low-quality schlock being printed and sold—especially in the business arena. Technology has made self-publishing really easy. Unfortunately, there's not much technology can do about the content quality of the books being published.

You don't want to be just another author.

You want to be an *extraordinary* author.

And you want to be a successful author.

That means you need to take some time to thoroughly plan out your book's journey before you start writing it. I'm not talking about outlines and chapters just yet. I'm talking about planning out what you want to happen with the book.

What are your goals for the book?
Who's going to read it?
What do you want your readers to do when they're finished?
Where do you plan to sell it?

Creating an extraordinary book is a little more work than simply slamming down a few thousand words on your computer and uploading them to Amazon. The extra attention to detail will pay off down the road.

Remember, this book will be your first introduction to many potential customers. As the saying goes, you never get a second chance to make a first impression. That's so true with books. If you take the time to create a book that truly serves your target audience, looks professional, and feels professional, you'll make a great first impression. When that happens, you'll find it's much easier to convert your readers into customers.

Planning is the first stage. Let's go through the things you need to consider when planning out how you're going to write your book. There will be plenty of other decisions down the road, but the considerations we're about to look at are essential to clarify before you start writing anything. If you've already started writing your book, consider taking some time to go back and do the necessary planning before writing any further.

I've created a special companion workbook you can download to help you through the entire book writing process. It's especially useful during the planning stage. So, if you haven't already downloaded it yet, go to www.TheProfitableBusinessAuthor.com/workbook, enter your name and email address, and you'll get instant access.

Chapter Two

## What's the Overall Goal (or Goals) for your book?

Before you begin writing, take some time to decide why you are writing this book. What's the end result you desire?

- To drive traffic to your website or generate more sales?
- To attract new clients to your service-based company?
- To open doors to speaking opportunities?
- To change people's lives or solve the world's problems?
- Or maybe you just want to leave a company legacy.

Now is the time to figure this out. Your goal will determine the content, structure, and organization of your book. Most authors go about this backward. They decide what they want to write about, and then try to make it work for their business. This is a ticket straight to Procrastination Land!

When you decide on your goal *before* you consider what to write, the writing comes much more easily. Here are some examples of possible goals you might have:

If your goal is to drive sales on a website, you need to mention the website address often and give readers a reason to go there.

If your goal is to build your mailing list, then you'll want to give away some additional free content readers can access when they join your list.

If your goal is to chronicle the history of your company and leave a legacy for the future, you might want to write a memoir-style book.

If you want to land speaking gigs, you will likely want to organize your book around your speaking topics.

Does that make sense?

Take some time to write down your goal or goals for your book. Use the workbook, or just write it in a notebook. You're going to refer to your goal(s) throughout the whole book-creation process.

Once you have your goal written down, it's time to imagine your readers.

## Who is Your Target Audience?

Not everyone will be interested in your book. Not everyone will be interested in your products or services, either. However, there is a natural audience for your book, and you'll need to think about them as you write. So, it's important to figure out exactly who you're writing for before you even create an outline. The audience you're writing for dictates what you write. Most likely, your readers are the same as your potential clients and customers.

If you're a grief counselor, your audience is people who have experienced loss. But what kind of loss, specifically? Do they need help coming to terms with the loss of a pet or a spouse? Are they adults or children? A book for children grieving over a lost parent will be completely different from a book about losing a beloved pet.

If your book teaches a system, are your target readers beginners or experts? Do they want a step-by-step guide or just an overview? Will they learn better from diagrams, photographs, or video demonstrations? What common pitfalls will they encounter?

If you're selling a product, does your target audience

understand what it does? Or will you need to explain it? Will your readers use the product themselves? Or will they buy it for others to use?

Your target audience will not only help you figure out your content, it will also help you figure out the style and tone of the book. For example, if your readers are over 40, they will expect a book to have lots of long paragraphs. They're probably used to reading, and generally don't mind big blocks of text. If your audience is younger, they will have a hard time with a book like that. Younger audiences, especially teenagers, have been trained by technology to read in short bursts. For these people, you'll want very short paragraphs, with lots of bullet points, charts, and pictures to break up the text.

Now it's your turn. Answer the following questions in your workbook or on paper. Don't just think about the answers, write them down.

- Who are your readers?
- What questions might they have?
- What problems might they have?
- How can you help them?
- Where do they hang out? (online and offline)
- Where do they shop?
- What magazines and movies do they enjoy?

## How to Read Your Readers' Minds

Too many authors decide what their books will be about without consulting or even thinking about their readers. You might know exactly what you want to write about, and that's okay. However, you're going to have an easier time selling your book if you consider what your readers want to know. Writing a book, especially a business book, is all about *serving the reader*. Look outside yourself and your own intimate knowledge of your business. Listen to what the market is asking for. Your target audience will tell you exactly what to write, if you'll only *pay attention*.

Here are a few ways to find out exactly what your readers want to know and decide what content you might want to include in your book. Not all of these suggestions will work for every situation or every book. However, they will certainly help you figure out what your audience wants to know, and what you might want to write about.

- Survey your customers. Ask them what they wish they had known before they purchased from you.
- Mine the FAQs (frequently asked questions) on your website. Those questions are pure gold for a book.
- Look through the online forums and social media groups in your industry to see what questions come up over and over. Facebook and LinkedIn groups are great places to start.
- Read reviews for books that are similar to yours. Pay attention to what people didn't like about other books on your topic. What did they feel was missing? Make sure you include those items in your book.
- Ask your salespeople questions like:
  - What are the most common questions you hear from prospects?
  - What's the hardest thing to explain?

- What do you wish prospects already knew coming into the sales conversation?
- What objections do you encounter over and over again?
- Ask your customer service people questions like:
  - What do customers complain about the most?
  - What do they wish was clearer?
  - What questions do you get over and over?

If you pay close attention, your customers and prospects will practically write the book for you. They will tell you exactly what they want to know. Then all you have to do is write out the answers to their questions and solve their problems. The hard part for many authors seems to be listening. They think they know exactly what they want their book to be about, but they don't consider what their readers really want to know. Don't be that author. Pay attention to your target readers.

## Are You Writing the Right Book for Your Business?

Sometimes authors get ideas in their heads for books that actually have nothing to do with their overall goals. For example, I recently collaborated with a coaching client who wanted to leave her corporate job and start her own training company. She was a well-regarded public speaking coach who enjoyed helping people feel more comfortable creating presentations and delivering them on stage. But when she came to me, she wanted to write a book on female empowerment.

What? I was completely confused.

She told me she had no idea how to get her book out of her head and onto the page. She just couldn't understand why she was having such a hard time getting started. The reason was simple: her business goals and her book topic didn't align. She needed to write a book like *How to Nail Your Next Presentation*, not one about women's issues. She was writing the wrong book for her goals at the time. Once I pointed that out, and she changed direction to address her customers' needs, all the pieces just naturally fell into place.

Another client came to me with a goal of becoming a motivational speaker on the topic of drive and determination. However, he wanted to write a mystery-style narrative. Now, that narrative book may have contained elements of drive and determination, but his plan for the book didn't really lead him any closer to his goal of speaking on stage. Once we outlined a book based on his speaking topics, and sprinkled in stories from his life, he had a great book that positioned him perfectly for a career as an expert on harnessing your drive to reach your dreams.

This is why it's so important to know *why* you're writing your book (your goal), and *who* you're writing it for (your target audience). When would-be authors don't know where to start, or feel stuck, they're often trying to write the wrong book. Once you've got your book subject, target audience, and overall business goals in alignment, things tend to move along more smoothly. Then it's time to decide what type of book you're going to write.

Chapter Two

## What Type of Book Should You Write?

Choosing the right kind of book is one of the most important planning steps. Let's review the most common types of business books.

**Prescriptive nonfiction:** This is your basic "how to" book. You're teaching the reader how to do something, such as selling a house, building a business, or moving through the grieving process. Most businesses can use this type of book quite effectively, especially if they sell services.

**Guidebook:** If you have a local business, you could write a guidebook about your town, state, or region. Naturally, you would include your business as a resource. If you own a bike shop, for example, you could write a book about the best trail rides in your area. If you run a restaurant, you could write a book on local cuisine.

**Allegory:** An allegory tells a story that illustrates a point, which then ties in to your business. These can be tricky to write, but if you enjoy telling stories and writing fiction, this might be a natural fit for you. If you're a coach or consultant, you might find an allegory demonstrates your core philosophy better than a typical nonfiction book. One example is *The Go-Giver* by Bob Burg and John David Mann. It's a fictional story that illustrates many business principles. (It's an amazing read, too. If you haven't read it, put it on your list!)

**Memoir:** A memoir is the story of a memory or experience you went through at some point in your life. Sometimes this type of book is called a biography. You don't need to tell your entire life's story, just the parts that make a certain point or tie in with a theme. In a business context, memoirs are often used by CEOs or successful entrepreneurs who relate their journeys to building their businesses. Some examples include *Delivering Happiness*, by Tony Hsieh, *Losing My Virginity*, by Richard Branson, and *Made in America*, by Sam Walton. If your goal is to attract speaking engagements or leave a company legacy, a memoir may be just the ticket for you.

**Direct sales piece:** If you sell products or services with long sales cycles, like major machinery, your book could be a long sales presentation. As long as you don't bore the reader, you can include all kinds of information about your product and its benefits. You can even overcome common sales objections right within the book. Think of the book as the education phase of your sales process. If you have major competitors, having a book that supports your business can mean the difference between making a sale and losing out to another company.

Very often the lines between genres of books get blurred. So, don't worry if the book you have in mind doesn't fit perfectly within a particular style. You just want a general idea for the type of book you're going to write. Take a few minutes to figure out how well your book aligns with your business goals, and decide which type of book suits your goals best. Write it down in your workbook.

## Should Your Book be an Ebook or Printed?

People often ask me if they really need a printed book. After all, the whole world is going digital, right? Don't underestimate the power of print! A printed book tells the reader *this is real*. Just like hardcover books still *feel* more important than paperbacks, printed books feel more important than ebooks.

## Chapter Two

The problem with ebooks is they read like web pages. Psychologically, they just don't have the same gravitas as a printed book. However, ebooks do offer convenience, portability, and low cost. I believe it's important to have your book available in both print and electronic formats. Fortunately, modern publishing options, including print-on-demand, make this easy and affordable.

### What About Audiobooks?

Is your customer more likely to listen to a book than to read it? I wouldn't advise producing an audio book exclusively, but it can be a great alternative to reading an existing printed book. People need to see that a printed version is available, so they know it's a "real" book. But then you can give them the option to consume the book the way they want to: printed, online as an ebook, or as an audio recording.

One strategy is to offer the audio version free with another purchase. You want your customers to actually consume the content, right? So give them the option to listen instead of read. It's tough to get "found" in the audio book world. Audio books are gaining popularity, and some people love them. However, readers usually hear about a book first, and then go looking for the audio version. The bottom line is that it doesn't hurt to offer as many options as you can. Audio books are often significantly more expensive, which means more money in your pocket, too.

Some authors are comfortable reading their own audio books, especially if they are professional speakers. However, many other authors hire voice artists to record the audio book for them. Either way is acceptable.

## Preliminary Title

People frequently tell me, "I'm thinking of writing a book; it's called _____."

They already know the title of their book. It's something they've been thinking about for a long time, maybe years, maybe decades. They are *married* to the title. They think it completely encapsulates everything they want to say. It's their message. It's their baby. And it's probably the wrong title.

Here's a tip that could save your sanity: Don't get emotionally attached to anything surrounding your book. Not the title, not the cover design, not the content. Do get emotionally attached to the outcomes and transformations you provide for your clients and customers. Get involved with their struggles. Be passionate about helping them reach their desired results.

A title has a job to do. And guess what? Its job is *not* to convey your message.

Its job is to attract attention and get potential readers to pick up your book.

Its job is also to be memorable, so people will pass it on through word of mouth.

Its job might also be to be visible in a search engine like Amazon.

A book title does its job partly through careful application of keywords and key phrases.

If you've done any work with search engine optimization (SEO) or pay-per-click (PPC) advertising, you're familiar with the importance of keywords. These are words and phrases your target audience uses every day on search engines like Google and Amazon to search for solutions. Solutions you may be able to provide. If your title matches the keywords your target audience is using, your book has a better chance of being discovered.

If you're writing a book about dog grooming businesses, for example, some possible key search phrases might include:

"How to start a dog grooming business"

"Marketing for groomers"

"Successful pet groomers"

If you want your title to be noticed by your target readers and found more easily on search engines, you should use as many of these key words as possible. Include combinations of the keywords in your title and subtitle. So, for the example above, some possible titles might be:

*Grooming Success: Marketing and Business Strategies for Dog Groomers*

*The Dog Biz: How to Start a Successful Dog Grooming Business in 6 Weeks*

Notice how these titles include lots of keywords and tell the reader exactly what the book is about. Don't be too clever or cryptic here. It's important to think strategically about your title, and be willing to change it as you progress through the writing stage. Choose a working title for now, but realize it might not make the final cut.

How do you know which keywords your target audience is using?

I've created a video showing you the easy way to find

this out using sites like Amazon, YouTube, and Google. You can find it on the resource page on the website: www.TheProfitableBusinessAuthor.com/resources.

## Some things to consider when choosing a title include:

- Amazon keywords: How many searched-for terms are in your title? You don't *have to* use keywords in your title, but it's a good idea to fit some in if possible.
- Branding: How does it fit with your current branding? Will customers be confused? If your title and cover match your branding, there is a nice sense of continuity that carries over from the book to your products and services. One way to use your branding in your title is to add a line above the title that says something like "Brand XYZ Presents" or "Presented by XYZ Company".
- Recognition: Will your target market know this book is for them? It might be a good idea to mention your target audience in the title, so they know it's for them. For example, *Accounting for Small Businesses*, *Family Walks in Maine*, or *The Puppy Owner's Guide to Obedience Training*.
- Results: Does the title make a bold promise? Tell the reader what the main benefit is. What will they learn if they read this book? For example, *How to Write a Book That Attracts Clients and Customers*, *How to Win Friends and Influence People*, or *Think and Grow Rich*.
- Uniqueness: Does the title stand out somehow? Is it funny, shocking, or memorable? A good title is eye-catching. For example, *How to Not Suck at Writing*, *Change or Die*, or *Freakonomics*.

Take some time to write down the important keywords

associated with your business. Then brainstorm some titles that might work.

## Start Thinking About a Cover Now

Typically, authors don't start thinking about a cover design until the end of the process, after the manuscript is finalized. But there are several good reasons to get a preliminary cover design before you even start writing, especially for self- or indie-published business books.

Authors will tell you that, once they have a cover design, the book finally feels *real*. Well, why would you wait until the end of the process for that? When you can see your book in a 3-D image, with a professional looking cover, the psychological benefits are huge. If it feels real, you're more likely to finish the writing and get on to the publishing stage. Just having an image of your book in front of you can help you move forward faster.

Another benefit of having a cover design early on is that the book can actually attract new clients and customers well before it's finished. You can post the cover image on your website or in your email signature. You can collect pre-orders. And when you say you are the "author of the upcoming book _____", people subconsciously equate that to you being a published author. It's like the expert status and positioning happens early because potential customers can *see* your book.

At this stage, it doesn't matter if you have the final title or cover design. It only matters that you have a *working* title and cover. Your final version will probably look quite different, and that's okay. It doesn't negate the benefits of having that cover image early.

Once you get closer to needing a final title and cover design, you can ask your followers on social media which ones they like best. This is a great engagement strategy that gets others involved in the project. When your followers feel like they have some input, they may be more likely to purchase your book when it's finished. They're also more likely to spread the word to friends and family.

So how do you get a preliminary cover design? If you're looking for a bargain design, you can find freelance designers on UpWork.com or 99Designs.com. You can also search for book cover designers on Google. Look for someone who has worked in your genre before. Check out their samples and make sure you like their style of design. Also, be sure their designs look professional and would look right at home on a bookstore shelf with other books in your genre.

## How to Get Endorsements

Another consideration to think about now is who you can ask to provide endorsements, a foreword, or back cover blurbs. People buy books that other people recommend. So, you want to have endorsements on your cover and inside the book whenever possible. Ideally, these blurbs will come from celebrities or well-known names. People your readers respect.

Recently, I ghostwrote a book for a well-respected Internet marketer. Even though he is a celebrity in his own right, he found other high-visibility people to endorse the book. Dan Kennedy (author and highly respected entrepreneur) wrote the foreword and Tony Robbins (world-famous motivational speaker) gave a back-cover blurb. Neither one of those endorsements would have been possible if we'd waited until the last minute to ask. People are busy, and it can sometimes take months to get even a two- or three-sentence endorsement. So, prepare for it now.

Who do you know? If you're good friends with some household names in your industry, great! Even if you don't know any industry celebrities in person, maybe someone in your network does. LinkedIn is a great resource for finding people who can introduce you to others. Perform a search on LinkedIn for your desired connection, then LinkedIn will give you a list of people in your network who may be able to provide a warm introduction.

Planning your endorsements now gives you some time to approach celebrities you don't know. Maybe you're writing a book about basketball, and you'd really love to get Michael Jordan to write a blurb about it. If you have a few months to get an introduction or find some way to connect with him, you have a much better chance than if you make a last-minute request.

Take some time to write down your dream list of endorsements. Who do you already know? And who would you love to find an introduction to? Dream big at this stage! You never know what can happen.

## How to Pre-Sell Readers on Your Expertise

There are three elements to include in your book that will help people transition from readers to clients or customers. The first element is *seeding*. You want to plant little "seeds" throughout the book that let readers know you are in business to help people just like them. These mentions are like little seeds that can grow into large accounts over time.

Talk about your clients. Talk about programs and products you are selling. Talk about the do-it-yourself services and done-for-you services you offer. But don't overdo this. It's meant to be subtle. You're not selling anything; you're just dropping hints now and then. You can write things like, "Most of my clients like to do it this way…" or "In my coaching program, 90% of students use this technique successfully."

The second element that turns readers into clients and customers is what I call *a three-dimensional call to action (3-D CTA)*. In the old days, books were two-dimensional. There were two ends to the book: the author and the reader. There was no easy way for the reader to get in touch with the author and ask questions. If they worked really hard, readers could find the author and maybe they would become a client. But the reader had to be extremely motivated to take those extra steps.

It's much better if the author has control of the contact. As the author, you want a natural, easy, low-pressure way to contact everyone who's bought your book so you can offer them other products and services. That's the 3-D CTA.

You'll need a website, an email list, and some relevant content that's not in the book. This extra content can be in a video or audio format--information that isn't easily conveyed in written form, and it should be extremely valuable to the reader.

For example, if your book is about starting a dog grooming business, you might tell the reader they can get access to a video that walks them step-by-step through the process of setting up a website. All they need to do to access this extra content is give you their name and email address. They are signing up for your email list by accessing this valuable extra. So now, instead of a 2-D relationship (author and reader), you have a 3-D relationship (author, reader, and website).

Once you have a reader's email address, you have control of the conversation. You can send them emails, make offers, and give them assistance and encouragement. There are all kinds of things you can do once you have that email address. This is how you get around the problem of not knowing who bought your book. The readers who are interested in building a relationship with you and your company will let you know by signing up for your list.

The third element to help convert readers to customers is a *high-value bonus* (HVB), which you add as a gift for people who buy the book. If you provide a lot of value in your bonus, you can attract clients and customers who never even buy your book. They might just happen to see it on Amazon and decide to take you up on the offer without buying the book. This is okay! The goal is to get them on your mailing list.

A high-value bonus can be a webinar that you present later; maybe it's video training or a half-hour consultation. It can be anything you like, as long as it's valuable to your target audience. Help them solve the biggest problems they have, and you'll win loyal followers.

Once you know what you want to offer, dedicate an entire page to this bonus within the first few pages of your book. Be sure to include a short description of the offer and the web address (URL) where it can be accessed.

The reason you want this offer page in the beginning of the book is so people browsing on Amazon will see it when they click on the *Look Inside* feature. Sometimes browsers will click over to your website to get the free offer, even if they don't wind up buying the book. You will request their name and email address to gain access to the bonus, which means you get another subscriber on your list. Once they're on your list, you can talk to them, build a relationship, and make other offers. Pretty cool, huh?

So, to pre-sell your readers, include seeding, one or more 3-D CTAs, and a high-value bonus in the front of your book. Start planning out what these will be so you can have the corresponding web pages created as you're writing. You're going to want all these offers ready to go when the book is published.

Take some time to write down what these various offers and bonuses might be. Keep in mind they could be products or services you currently offer. You don't always have to create something brand new.

## Plan Out Your Budget

There's an old saying among consultants: *Cheap, Fast, or Good: Pick two*. That goes for book as well. If your goal is to create an excellent book, you're going to have to pay for it either in time or money. Paying for it in time means you write it, you figure out how to publish it yourself, and you do all the marketing and publicity. This is fine, but it's going to take a long time, and you might not have the same distribution options as if you spent some money on outside help.

Even if you're doing most of the publishing work yourself, you will have expenses related to the book. Estimates for the cost of self-publishing, distributing, and marketing a book can run as high as $20,000! This is why it's so important to plan how you're going to get a return on your investment early in the process. It's easier to spend that kind of money when you have a plan in place to bring you hundreds of thousands of dollars in return.

You may wind up needing to pay for some or all of the following:

- Advertising or publicity consultant
- Copy editor
- Cover designer
- Distribution consultant
- Fact checker
- Ghostwriter
- Indexer
- Interior layout designer
- ISBN and bar code
- Marketing consultant
- Publishing consultant
- Structural editor

Many companies offer several of these services under one roof. And there are workarounds to help keep the costs as low as possible. Weigh the cost of producing your book against the possible clients and customers you could gain because of it, then set your budget accordingly.

For example, if you sell large machinery or offer executive consulting that costs well into the mid-six figures, then attracting just one client from your book could make it worth your while. In that case, it might be smart to invest $150,000 or so to hire a high-level, professional business ghostwriter and pay a book coach or indie publisher to produce the book for you. You'll be assured of a top-notch final product, and you'll have an evergreen sales piece that works for you year in and year out. The best part is that you'll still make a return on your investment with the first sale.

On the other hand, if you're a mom-and-pop local gift shop, and your average customer only spends about $20 in your store, it might make more sense to go with a tighter budget. Maybe you purchase some done-for-you design templates, get a cover created at 99Designs, and save most of your budget for editing and publicity. Just because you go with a less expensive option doesn't mean you can't have a top-quality book. You'll just have to put in a little more elbow grease yourself.

By now, you have laid some significant groundwork, and you're ready to start writing. Take a moment and be proud of the work you've accomplished so far. You're already way ahead of authors who slap together their books in a weekend and then wonder why they don't make a profit.

If you haven't already, download the companion workbook and fill it out. The time you take planning your book now will save you significantly more time down the road.

Are you eager to get started?

Let's take a look at the writing process next.

Chapter Two

# CASE STUDY

**Life After Debt:**
**Practical Solutions To Get Out of Debt, Build Wealth, And Radically Transform Your Finances Forever!**
By Rob Kosberg

**Author's business:** Financial services at the time of the book's publication; currently, BestSellerPublishing.org
**Target market:** Entrepreneurs and business owners

**Tell us about your book.**
*Life After Debt* is the culmination of thousands of one-on-one meetings with people deep in debt. I peel back the curtain on the strategies and mindset needed to overcome debt once and for all.

**Why did you decide to write a book?**
My goal was to rebrand myself as a thought leader in the financial services industry. I knew that writing a book would be the first step in achieving that. I was overwhelmed with the success of the book. *Life After Debt* became an Amazon #1 best-selling book across several categories and has sold over 35,000 copies to date.

**How did you find the writing process?**
Slow and painful! I paid thousands of dollars for the book to be written by a ghostwriter, but was so unhappy with the end result from that particular writer that I threw that version away and started over myself from scratch. It took me approximately 18 months to complete.

**Did the book help you achieve your goal?**
Within 15 months of launching *Life After Debt*, I was asked to do my own radio show, resulting in four hours of live radio per week, which helped to produce over a million dollars of income.

Writing *Life After Debt* completely changed my life, and having it become a best-seller opened up tremendous doors for me. Since its publication date, I have founded Best Seller Publishing, performed numerous speaking engagements and been featured on ABC, CBS, NBC, FOX, and the *Wall Street Journal*.

People were constantly asking me how I had achieved all of this and sought advice on how they could do the same. In 2011, I opened the doors to my new business, Best Seller Publishing, a unique publishing house that devotes itself to helping people from all walks of life become best-selling authors, launching them towards a life of independence, meaningful impact, and financial freedom by using their books as marketing tools.

# Chapter Three

## Writing

Almost every day, I receive messages from people struggling to write their books. Either they don't know how to get started, or they're stuck and don't know why. Often the solution for both problems is the same: an *effective* outline.

That's it. The big secret! Knowing how to construct a useful outline is what makes professionals stand out from would-be authors.

What's the big deal? Everyone knows you need an outline, right?

The problem is that very few people have ever been taught how to write an outline that actually carries them through the writing. One that keeps them moving forward so they never get stuck. And one that helps them sell the book once it's published.

You probably learned how to outline in elementary school. Your teacher may have told you that an outline creates organization. Maybe you learned how to write an introduction to tell people what you were going to write about, then maybe you had to write three paragraphs making a point in each one, and then you wrote a conclusion where you summarized the previous three paragraphs.

Sound familiar?

You probably learned how to write an outline that used Roman numerals, capital letters, numbers, and lowercase letters. And it was just a crazy formatting nightmare. If your teachers were anything like mine, they were probably more interested in the format of your outline than the actual content.

If you hate writing outlines, and you're having terrifying flashbacks to junior high school, I want you to completely forget about it. Just erase it from your brain.

Fortunately, that is not the kind of outline I'm talking about!

When I say "outline", I'm talking about a writing aid. Something that actually helps you write your book, and organizes the content so it makes sense for your readers. An effective outline helps you convey all the information the readers need in order to benefit from the book *and* to take the next step.

Maybe the next step you want readers to take is subscribing to your list or following you on social media. Maybe you want them to buy your products, or services. Whatever you want the readers to do, you can help them take that next step by creating a useful outline.

That's it.

No Roman numerals. No crazy formatting.

Many writers will jot down a list of bullet points they think they should talk about, and figure they'll just "wing it" from there. They believe a short, simple list of ideas will be enough of a prompt to keep them writing. After all, they can talk for hours

## Chapter Three

about real estate investing without notes in front of them. Why would they need a list of notes in order to write about it?

Once they start writing, however, they discover something different. They soon see that their bullet-point list isn't sufficient, not because they don't know what to write, but because there's *too much* to write! They know so much about the topic, they freeze when they see a vague bullet point on the screen.

Staring back at them.

Taunting them.

Daring them to keep writing.

If they don't freeze, they might go to the other end of the spectrum and just spew out everything they know about one particular topic. The writing makes no sense because it's not organized. They don't know when to stop. Either way, the writer is stuck.

On the other hand, the kind of outline I'm going to show you actually pulls you forward. You don't get stuck because the outline feeds you exactly what to say next. And when that happens, you're able to write in small chunks of time without getting lost. Very few writers, even professional writers, can sit down and compose text for four hours straight. That's really difficult and takes a lot of training and dedication (not to mention four hours of free time).

But when you have a kick-ass outline, you never have to dedicate hours at a time. Even if you only have twenty minutes a day to write, you can still make progress! (Sounds pretty awesome, doesn't it?)

I hope I've convinced you that you need to rethink how you put together an outline. Are you ready to learn how to do it?

## The Secret to a Great Outline is Great Questions

You get answers by asking questions, right? The human brain is wired to search for answers when it sees questions. We can't help it. So, you build an effective book outline by asking lots of questions in a logical sequence.

You can start your outline by writing a list of bullet points that cover the topics you want to write about, that's fine. But then you need to turn those bullets into a detailed list of questions. Not just any questions, but ones that your readers most likely already have (or should have) about a certain topic.

**Which outline items below would be easier to write from?**
How to start investing
OR
What does a beginner need to get started in the stock market?
When should a person start thinking about investing?
Where is the best place to get educated about stocks?
Who can you trust to give good advice?

Buying the perfect house
OR
What considerations go into buying the perfect house?
How can you find a great neighborhood that suits your personality?
What time of year is best for house hunting?
Is there really such a thing as a "perfect" house?

## Chapter Three

Maintaining your bicycle
OR
What kinds of regular maintenance are important for a mountain bike?
When there's a problem with a bike, should the rider fix it or take it to a shop?
What kinds of modifications are available to make a tricked-out bike?
How do you keep the paint job looking fresh?
How do you keep the gears running smoothly?

Do you see how simply framing the general topic in the form of several specific questions makes it easier to start writing? Once you have the questions framed in your outline, the writing is a simple matter of answering your own questions.

Your brain is wired to answer questions. Any time you read a question, your brain automatically starts searching for the answer. So, when your outline is entirely composed of questions about your topic, you never get stuck wondering what to write next. Your brain just naturally kicks in.

### How to Create Effective Questions

The key to asking good questions is to use interrogatives. An interrogative is just a word that starts a question. So, your outline items should begin with words like who, what, when, where, why, how, how much, which ones, can you, etc.

For example:
Who should _____ and why?
What are the best practices for _____?

When should you _____?
Why do _____ do _____?
Can you _____ when _____?
How do you _____?

You can also turn some or all questions into negatives, if you'd like.

Who shouldn't _____?
What mistakes should you avoid when _____?
When is it impossible or unwise to _____?
Where should you never _____?
Why should you never _____ when _____?

Do you see how this works?

If you get stuck, just look at the topic and list these interrogatives in your head, one at a time. Who. What. When. Where. Why. The questions will start to form themselves. Remember, you want to get inside the heads of your readers. Ask the questions they are likely already wondering about. You may be tempted to skip the more basic questions because you want to look like an expert. Don't! Answer the readers' most pressing questions on the topic, even if they seem obvious to you.

## Creating Your Outline is a Simple Three-Step Process

**Step 1:** Decide on the overall theme of the book.
**Step 2:** Brainstorm a list of topics you plan to cover or chapters you think make sense. Write these out in bullet point format, making sub-lists as necessary.

**Step 3:** List those topics in a logical order and start filling them in with questions.

Let's go back to the dog grooming book example from the previous chapter. Imagine you're a dog groomer and your book is about helping other people start their own dog grooming businesses. That's the overall theme.

Next, brainstorm your topics or chapters. This is where your bullet point list comes in.

- Learning how to groom
- Finding a location
- Setting up the business
- Getting clients

That's a decent few chapters, but the topics are way too broad. If you start writing your book from there, you're going to get stuck. There's too much you could write about, and not enough direction. So, break the general topics down into questions.

**Learning How to Groom**
How did you (the author) learn dog grooming?
Who should be a dog groomer? And who should not?
What does a typical day look like?
Is it a physically demanding job?
Are there dog-grooming schools?
Do you need a formal education, or can you just practice on your dog at home?
Are certifications a good idea?
How long does it take to learn?
How can you keep up with popular styles and products?

How many hours should you practice?
How many types of dogs should you practice on?

**Finding a Location**
How important is location to the success of your business?
What makes a good location?
What makes a bad location?
How much square footage do you need?

**Setting Up Your Business**
What legal paperwork do you need to file?
What equipment do you need, at a minimum?
What additional equipment should you consider?
How much does it cost to get the business up and running?
What are good hours to keep?
Do you need to stay open on the weekends?
Are there slow seasons?
Should you also consider grooming other animals?

**Getting Clients**
What are the best marketing strategies for groomers?
Should you advertise online or offline, or both?
How can you partner with similar businesses like pet shops?
How can you encourage referrals?
How can you turn a one-time customer into a regular?
Should you specialize in a particular breed?

That sounds like a pretty good book on how to start a grooming business, don't you think? And I could keep adding dozens more questions, if I needed to. The more questions you ask, the easier your writing will be. So, just keep asking questions until you've exhausted the topic. If you're concerned about having too much content, you can always go back later and edit out some of the less important topics. Also, realize that the more questions you have, the less you may need to write for each one.

In case you're not convinced you should take the time to create a question-based outline (QBO), let's look at some more benefits of writing this way.

## Your QBO is an Amazing Sales Tool

The outline becomes your table of contents. You can use it practically verbatim, including all the questions. Remember, those questions are exactly the same ones your target readers probably have about the topic. By leaving the questions in the table of contents, you help sell your book. When a potential buyer picks up your book and sees those questions, it piques her curiosity. Inside her head, she's thinking, "Heck yeah, I need this book. It answers all my questions!" This is why books are great positioning tools. You are the one with the answers, so you are considered the expert.

In addition to the table of contents, you can use your best question sets on the back cover of your book to encourage people to buy it. You can also put these questions on your website or in your Amazon book description. You can use them in a video book trailer. You can use them as talking points to get radio or TV publicity. You can answer them as snippets on YouTube videos. When you create a great QBO, your marketing work is half done. It's a beautiful thing!

## Your QBO Allows You to Write in Tiny Chunks of Time

One of the biggest objections I get when I tell people they should write a book is "I don't have time!!" I completely understand. I'm a businessperson, too. However, when you take the time to create a question-based outline, it breaks the book into bite-sized pieces that you can handle in short bursts.

So rather than thinking, "Sheesh! I have to sit down and write 10,000 words today," you think, "Ok, all I have to do is answer a question or two."

If you create a long enough list of questions, you may only need about ten or fifteen minutes to answer one of them. If you're taking longer than 30 minutes, you might want to go back and see if you can break that question down into more questions. After all, this is your business. You are an expert at what you do. Imagine a potential client walked up to you and asked that exact question. Most likely, it wouldn't take you a half-hour to answer. You might decide to answer one question or three in a single writing session. The point is, you can make progress on your book even if you only have ten or fifteen minutes at a time to work on it.

## Your QBO Keeps You Moving Forward

Breaking your book down into lots of questions creates milestones, so you have little successes along the way. Every time you finish answering a question, you can say, "Sweet! I did that one, now I can do the next one." So the outline becomes a tool that keeps you moving forward. It makes you feel successful, so you want to keep going. When you don't have the right kind of outline, it's really easy to get stuck and become completely frustrated.

Using a QBO also lets you write out of sequence without losing your mind. Maybe you don't feel like writing about topic A today; you're just not in the mood. But topic C is really exciting you. It's on your mind, you had a dream about it, and you just want to run with it. You can do that when you have a question-based outline. You don't have to start at page one and write straight through to the end. You can jump around and cover different topics when you feel like it.

## Your QBO Creates Marketing Content Automatically

When you build your outline using questions, you're able to write your book, your marketing content, and your platform-building materials all at the same time. This is the secret that lets certain authors have massive social media campaigns that seem to appear everywhere at once. They're on YouTube, they're on Twitter, they're on LinkedIn, and on Facebook—they're all over the place.

How do they do that? Each question in your outline becomes multiple pieces of content as it is answered fully. Maybe a group of questions becomes a blog post. Then you break them down for short YouTube videos. You pull out quotes to add to pictures and infographics on Twitter and Instagram. Dissect your book into bits and pieces of content, then link that content to someplace a reader can buy the complete book. Pretty cool, huh?

There's one more thing you should consider when you're creating your outline, and that's your framework.

## How Do You Build a Framework?

A framework is just an organizational structure to hang your chapters on. It helps readers follow along and know where they are in the process. It also helps the readers organize the content in their brains. Frameworks and outlines are kind of chicken and egg scenarios. Some authors create the framework first, and others need an outline in order to see the framework. Either way you do it is fine.

For example, in *The Seven Habits of Highly Effective People* by Steven Covey, the framework is the seven habits. It's easy to follow along, and the readers know they're done when they get to number seven.

The framework is simply a way for the book to flow naturally and make sense. There are lots of different ways to develop a framework for your book. Here are a few ideas:

- A coaching book might have six steps to success.
- A local hiking guide might be organized by region, or by difficulty (easy/moderate/difficult hikes).
- A recipe book might be organized by meal category: breakfast, lunch, dinner, dessert, snacks.
- A diet book might be organized by quick start/phase 1/phase 2/maintenance.
- A book about real estate might be organized by before/during/after the sale.

Do you see how this works? You want your content to fall into some sort of recognizable pattern, whether it's sequential, regional, seasonal, geographical, or some other pattern you think makes sense. The trick is to make it familiar to the reader. As you may have noticed, the framework for the book you're reading now is sequential; it leads you through the stages of creating a book in order.

Take a look back at your outline, and see if you created a framework without realizing it. Many people do, simply because they read a lot, and books are typically built on frameworks. If your content appears scattered or disorganized, see if there's a way you can rearrange it to fit a familiar framework. You're not looking to be creative or original here; you simply want your audience to follow along easily. When they are able to do that, they comprehend the material better. And the better they comprehend, the more likely they are to put the information to use in their lives.

## 19 Nonfiction Book Elements to Consider Including in Your Book

The QBO makes up the bulk of your book. However, you don't want your book to sound like just a Q&A session. So, you'll want to sprinkle certain other elements into your manuscript where they make sense. Every now and then, you'll want to include a story. Sometimes you'll need examples or a list of options for the reader to choose from. You may want to put action steps at the end of every chapter.

Below are some of the most common nonfiction elements. Use them like herbs and spices throughout your book. Mix and match them. Some of them you'll want in every chapter. Some will only make sense occasionally. And some may not be necessary at all.

You are the boss of your book! You get to create the chapters however you want to. Which means you can use some, all, or none of these elements. It's up to you. Read through the nineteen elements below, then I'll show you how to combine them together in your book.

**1. Stories**
- Client case studies and testimonials
- Fictional stories made up to illustrate a point
- Personal anecdotes
- Popular movies or legends that relate to your book

**2. Practice Exercises**
- Fill-in-the-blank
- Journaling exercises
- Physical exercises
- Workbooks

**3. Action Steps**
- What do they need to do?
- In what order?

**4. Common Mistakes to Avoid**
- Where do people often get tripped up?
- How can they work toward a more successful outcome?

**5. Setting the Problem**
- Describe the readers' frustrations
- What does their typical day look like?
- What are their problems
- Paint a vivid picture

6. **Presenting Your Solution and Future Pacing**
    - Help the readers see what their lives could be like.
    - "Imagine what it would be like if . . ."
7. **Uniqueness**
    - How is this book different from any other book on the subject?
    - How is your system or your product unique?
    - What extra services do you offer that your competitors don't?
    - How do you go the extra mile for your customers?
8. **Outside Resources**
    - Where else can they get help?
    - Are there other books you recommend?
    - Are there other (non-competing) experts you recommend they study?
9. **Offers**
    - Your company's relevant offers
    - 3-D Call to Action
    - High-Value Bonus
10. **Quotations**
    - From celebrities or well-known people in your industry
    - From you
    - From clients or customers
11. **Step-by-Step Instructions**
    - Explanation of a process or system
    - Walk-through of a journey to a certain outcome
12. **Lessons and Advice**
    - What's the lesson to be learned in this chapter?
    - What advice should the reader pay close attention to?

### 13. Examples
- Use examples to illustrate a point. Well-known examples make your point easier to understand and lend credibility.
- Contrasting examples are helpful, too. Tell the reader what something is like, and what it is not like.

### 14. Lists
- Bulleted or numbered lists of choices, options, or examples.
- Ordered lists of steps or unordered random samplings.

### 15. Images
- Photographs, illustrations, charts, graphs, info-graphics
- Be sure to carefully check copyright laws.

### 16. Backstory and Credibility Builders
- Who are you and why should we believe what you're saying?
- What's your experience in the industry?
- These can be in the form of stories.

### 17. Summaries
- Sum up the chapter as a review.
- Consider making them stand out in boxes or with sub-headlines.

### 18. Ratings and Reviews
- For guidebooks especially, rate the trails or the recipes to help the reader make a more informed choice.
- If you're writing about walking trails, you could rate them by how challenging they are.
- If you're reviewing hot sauces from around the world, you could rate them by how spicy they are.

**19. Next Chapter Teaser**
- Give the reader a hint of what's coming up in the next chapter.
- Asking questions is a great way to get them to keep turning the pages.

## How to Combine These Elements in Your Book

Build the chapters in your book by mixing and matching these elements (or others you think of on your own). Your topic questions are the centerpieces of the chapter. Then you can sprinkle in the other elements where they make sense.

Some elements, like your background and credibility-builders might only make sense in the introduction. Or perhaps you don't want to overstate your qualifications, and prefer to use this element in the back of the book on a special "About the Author" page.

Some books may need "Common Mistakes to Avoid" at the end of every chapter, while others only need it at the end of the book or not at all.

You may want to drop special offers into your manuscript now and then, or you might not want to include any offers at all.

Do you see how this works?

It's like a book buffet! Just pick and choose which elements make sense. And when you're stuck for a transition between questions on your outline, just refer to this list. Very often, the right element will jump out and say, "Pick me! I'm perfect."

Below are several examples of combinations.

**Sample chapter:**

- You might start with a true story that's relevant to the first question in the chapter outline.
- Then lead into the question itself and give your answer.
- Then you may need to include an example of how the answer rings true in the real world.
- Throw in a relevant client testimonial.
- Then lead into the next question and answer.
- Then provide a step-by-step list for how the reader can achieve the same results.
- Then offer an infographic that lists all the steps in order.
- Summarize the chapter.
- Offer some action steps.
- Transition to the next chapter.

**Another sample chapter:**

- Start with an image that summarizes the chapter.
- Move into the first question and answer.
- Provide a real-world example.
- Give an exercise for the reader to practice.
- Tell a story.
- Move into the next question and answer.
- Provide an example.
- Give an exercise.
- Repeat until all the questions are finished for the chapter.
- Offer some mistakes to avoid.
- Transition to the next chapter.

**Yet another sample chapter:**

- Story
- Image
- Question/answer
- Image
- Question/answer
- Image
- Question/answer
- Summary
- Transition to next chapter

**Very simple chapter:**

- Personal story
- Instructions
- Quote from a celebrity

When you plan your chapters out this way, they begin to develop a rhythm. Well-written books have a natural pacing that keeps the reader moving along. They know where they are in the chapter (perhaps unconsciously) because you've *carefully crafted* the chapters to follow a certain predictable flow. Once you have a flow that works, try to stick close to it in every chapter. Repetition is what creates that nice natural flow.

If you're not sure which elements you should include, don't worry. Just write through your first draft. It's possible that you'll find places to fit stories and offers and such naturally as you're writing. If not, you can always go back during the first edit and consciously look for places to add elements.

Okay, it's time . . .
The moment of truth . . .

## It's time to dive in and start writing your book.

If you took the time to set up your framework and outline, the writing should flow fairly easily. If it doesn't, go back to your questions and see if you veered off course anywhere. Perhaps you need to break the questions down into even more specific questions.

Don't worry about how long your answers are. Just answer each question completely, then move to the next one. It's possible one answer might be only a few sentences, and others might run on for pages. That's okay. You're writing a first draft at this point. The first draft is going to be messy and imperfect. Don't worry about it. Just get the words down. You'll have time to make them perfect during the editing stage.

## Different Ways to Write a Book

As the saying goes, there's more than one way to skin a cat. (Why anyone would want to skin a cat, I have no idea.) The point is, if you want to write a book, there's more than one way to do that as well. The most obvious way is to sit down with your introduction or first chapter and start writing. *Once upon a time . . . It was a dark and stormy night . . . It was the best of times; it was the worst of times . . .*

Let me tell you right now, that is the slowest way to write a book! (And possibly the most frustrating, too.) There will

## Chapter Three

be times you get distracted or bored. And, if you're like most business people, you'll try to muscle your way through it with rigid determination. You'll try to force yourself to finish a certain number of words. Or you'll sit down at the end of a long workday and try to make yourself write for two hours.

That strategy is a recipe for disaster! You'll find reasons not to write. Your kids will need attention. All sorts of important emergencies will crop up in your business. And if you do manage to grit your way through an entire book, you'll be exhausted and may not have the energy to see the project all the way through to publication.

Now, this is just my personal experience after more than twenty years as a professional writer. You don't have to take my word for it. Some people really do work better when they write linearly; that is, from page one to "the end". So try it out, if you must. However, if you find yourself struggling, let yourself off the hook and learn to write in non-linear chunks.

Remember when I said a question-based outline would let you skip around and just address the questions you feel like answering? That's what I'm talking about here. It's the fastest way I've found to write anything, from a book to a sales letter to a blog post. If you're using writing software like Scrivener, you can set up folders for each chapter and add separate documents for each question in your outline. If you're using MS Word or some other software, just use regular folders and documents.

This is an important step because you won't have to feel guilty if you only write a couple of paragraphs at a time. Your only job is to answer the question at the top of each individual document. The more questions you have, the less you need to write for each one.

I find if I print out my outline and just sort of skim over it, there's always one question my brain latches onto, and it starts spitting out the words in response. It might not be what I was expecting to write that day. That's okay. I'm going with whatever works here. The best part is I can write my book in short chunks of time, like when I'm waiting to pick up my son after school. If you have a daily commute by train, just think how much writing you could accomplish using this strategy. We all have small chunks of time available during the day. Where could you carve out ten or fifteen minutes to make some progress on your book?

Don't waste time going back over your other answers.

Pick one question, open one document, and just answer the question.

## Speaking Your Book

Some folks just shouldn't write at all; they should speak their books instead. (Bear with me for a minute, okay?) Sometimes starting with a blank page, even with a brain-tickling question at the top, is just too daunting. It's too hard to translate thoughts on a subject to the written word. In this case, the solution might be to pull out your smart phone, or plug a microphone into any recording device, and speak your answers to your outline questions.

Answer each question as if you were talking to a customer over lunch. Then, send the recordings out to a transcriptionist. My favorite transcription service is Rev.com; they're fast, reliable, and reasonably priced. (Recordings typically only cost about $1 per minute.) Once you get the transcriptions back, you can move straight to the editing stage. It's almost like you skipped writing altogether.

However, *do not* publish directly from your transcription! I've seen people do this, and it's really embarrassing for them. A transcription is not the same as a book. That's because people speak differently than they read. Edit the transcription so it flows naturally to the reading eye. If you don't want to do the editing yourself, outsource it to a professional. Believe me, it's worth taking the extra time.

## BLOGGING YOUR BOOK

This is another great way to write your book in small chunks over time. Simply write up a series of blog posts on a topic and put them together to form a first draft of your book. If you've already got the posts written, it's a little harder to make them fit the question-based outline format. But, as long as they make sense within your framework, you can fudge it a little.

The benefit of blogging a topic before you publish is you get to see how your audience reacts. Did they understand what you were trying to say? Did they have more questions you didn't think of? Did they bring up an opposing point of view?

Blogging is a great way to test-drive your answers, but it can take significantly longer to get a finished product. If you already have a blog with a large loyal following, you might want to consider using some of your existing posts and filling in the rest of the book with original content.

## Crowdsourcing Your Book

Want all the benefits of being an author, but don't want to write the whole book yourself? Crowdsourcing might be a good option for you. This is a strategy where you get other people to contribute content for a book in return for co-author status, or for a mention somewhere in the book. This is a great way to fill content gaps, bulk up a thin section, or even write the entire book. (Some of the most successful books in history are written this way. Many of them start with *Chicken Soup For The_____.*)

There are several ways to crowdsource a book. You could get different industry experts to contribute chapters on their own areas of expertise. The best-selling book *Social Boom!* by Jeffrey Gitomer was written this way. The theme for that book is different ways to use social media in your business. Different social media experts each contributed and received full credit at the front of their respective chapters.

Another way to crowdsource book content is to scour forums and niche websites. The book *1,000 Clever Sewing Shortcuts and Tips: Top-Rated Favorites from Sewing Fans and Master Teachers* by Deepika Prakash was written this way. The owner of a popular sewing forum collected hundreds of short tips from her members and put them all into a book. Each contributor had their name published along with their tip.

You could also interview your clients and customers as case studies. Ask how they used your product or service to solve a particular problem. Case studies and testimonials are often used as filler for business books. And they serve another purpose: they pre-sell readers on your wonderful company. A good case study is a third-party endorsement. It's social proof. And it's also more pages in your book.

## Hiring a Ghostwriter

If you want the ultimate shortcut, you can hire a ghostwriter. While this seems like an easy way out of writing, you will still have to do some work. My ghostwriting clients are often surprised by how much work they still have to put in, even when they aren't doing the writing!

A great ghostwriter will do her best to make you sound amazing in your book. That means developing the best framework for your goals and target audience, getting all the facts straight, and finding your voice. You want a writer who will deliver an excellent book, one you're proud of and can use to promote your business for years to come. That means you need to have input during the process. Hiring a top-quality ghostwriter can mean the difference between years of struggling over your book and just getting it out there working for you as quickly as possible.

Even though I've given you all the tools, shortcuts, and encouragement I can in this book, you might still decide it's more cost-effective to hire a ghostwriter. If that's the case, I want to make sure you understand exactly how to hire the *right* ghostwriter for you. So, here are a few tips for hiring a great ghostwriter.

1. If they don't ask you, "What is the goal for this book?" at the beginning of your conversation, *run*, don't walk, away from the conversation. A good business ghostwriter understands that you're writing the book for a particular purpose, whether

it's client acquisition, prestige, status, or some other reason. Understanding your goals is critical to the success of the book.

2. If they don't ask, "Who is your target audience?" at the beginning of your conversation, again…run, don't walk, away from the conversation. It's equally critical that they know who you want to reach with the book.

3. Find out how they plan to write in your voice. An experienced ghostwriter knows how to do this, and can make sure the book sounds just like you wrote it yourself. Every business has its own culture, its own personality and quirks. If your book reads like it was written by a lawyer, and your brand is all about a living a laid-back surfer lifestyle, there will be a major mental disconnect between your readers and your company. Readers will innately feel there's something wrong if they try to make a purchase and the vibe is completely different from what they expect. This is especially important if you plan to do any public speaking. Event organizers will read your book and form expectations in their minds. If you deliver something completely different, it could be disastrous.

4. Obtain references and samples. You can ask a potential ghostwriter what they've worked on, but understand they may not be allowed to disclose their clients. (We are, after all, ghost writers. We get paid to be invisible.) However, they should be able to point you to references, testimonials, or their own books as proof of their writing ability and style. For example, some of my past clients are happy to speak with my prospects on the phone, but prefer that I don't advertise that I wrote their books.

5. Find out exactly what work they will do with your book. Most ghostwriters will write the book, go through the first round of editing with you, hand you the manuscript in MS Word, and then you're on your own!

When I work with clients, I write the book, develop a platform-building and marketing strategy, source artwork or illustrations, and help them through the editing and publishing stages. Sometimes I will go so far as to build their websites, develop sales funnels, and write email campaigns. I want your book to be as successful as possible. So, I work on a lot more than just writing the manuscript.

This is not typical! Most ghosts are writers, not marketers. Don't expect them to be able to execute a launch plan. Their involvement begins and ends with the manuscript. If you do find a ghost who can also handle the marketing side of things, pay them extremely well and give them frequent appreciation. They are worth their weight in gold!

6. Expect to pay mid-to-high five figures for a full-length book. Mid-range professional ghostwriters charge between $45,000 and $80,000. Experienced ghosts and those providing add-on publishing and marketing help can charge $100,000 and up.

This expense is why it's so important for you to know what kind of return-on-investment you expect on your book. How much money do you expect to make up on the back end? How easy will it be to distribute your book? Do you already have a large market to sell to?

If you're selling $50 widgets, you'll have to sell a lot of them to break even on the cost of a ghostwritten book. But if you're selling $50,000 consulting packages, or you're setting up $20,000 speaking engagements, it makes total sense to hire a high-level professional who will help you reach your goals as quickly as possible. One client of mine made a staggering return of over $800,000 in the first couple of months after launching his book!

7. Get the right kind of writer. There are all kinds of writers out there, and people often confuse the roles of content writers, copywriters, and ghostwriters.
- **Content writers** write articles, listicles, and other viral content designed as traffic-generators.
- **Copywriters** write sales messages, from pay-per-click ads to web content and email campaigns.
- **Ghostwriters** write books.

Also, different ghosts specialize in different types of writing. I mostly work with prescriptive nonfiction, how-to, and self-help. Others may work exclusively with memoir or sales letter books. Find a writer who is experienced in writing the kind of book you have in mind.

8. Consider negotiating a co-authorship. Most of the time, you will be the author of the book. But sometimes you'll see a book cover that looks like this:

TITLE<br>By "Big name author"<br>With "Other author"

The word "with" is a giveaway that the book was written by a ghostwriter. The co-author is frequently the ghost. If the book is going to be widely distributed, a ghost may sometimes lower their fees in return for being named as a co-author. It doesn't hurt to ask.

Where do you start looking for ghostwriters? Ask around. Do you know any authors? Find out if they wrote their books or hired writers. You may be surprised at how common it is to use a ghost. Another great place to look is LinkedIn. Professional writers will show up in a general search, and there are several groups for ghostwriters. You may be able to find the perfect ghost there.

Chapter Three

## Finding Your Unique Voice

Business books shouldn't be dry philosophical dissertations or boring explanations of your products and services. Remember, your reader can put the book down at any time. So, it needs to be interesting, helpful, valuable, entertaining, and full of personality.

You'll often hear writers talk about their "voice". What does that even mean, anyway? All it means is write like you talk. Stay true to yourself and write as authentically as possible. Do you normally use colorful language and tell outrageous stories when you're hanging out with your friends? How can you bring that personality to your book? Do you have a signature dialect or regional accent? Let it shine through. Make sure your voice aligns with your readers' expectations. You don't want to alienate people with too colorful language, if they're not expecting it.

One of the easiest ways to find your voice is to record it and listen to yourself. (Don't get hung up on how you sound, nobody else is listening.) Focus on your cadence and rhythm. Do you use long sentences or short ones? Do you use fancy words or industry jargon? Write like you talk, and you will write in your voice.

Don't underestimate your reader. She is smart and capable, and she's a real human being. She wants to interact with you through this book. She hears your voice in her head while she reads. If she thinks you're dry and boring, there's not much chance she'll want to do business with you. That doesn't mean you can't be serious, just don't be overly formal. You're not writing a 12th grade term paper, and your reader is probably not your English teacher.

Be yourself, m'kay?

## Images and Artwork

As you're writing, think about where you can add visual aids to complement the text. Pictures, graphs, charts, screenshots, cartoons, and illustrations are all great ways to break up miles of text and make a book easier to read. I like to include some form of image every few pages in my clients' books, whenever it's appropriate. After all, a picture is worth a thousand words. And sometimes visuals can explain a concept more quickly and easily than words can.

Be aware that you'll need permission to use images taken from the Internet, or from anywhere else, for that matter. If you own the copyright—meaning you took the photo, commissioned the illustration, or licensed the image in some way—then you're fine. But you can't just take a screenshot of a competitor's website and use it in your book without written permission.

Some large websites like Google and Amazon have blanket permission forms for certain types of pictures. Just be sure you know who owns the rights before you put these graphics into your book. If you do need to seek written permission, the sooner you ask, the better. It can take months of searching before you find the right person to give you the go-ahead. And publishers require these written permissions before they will accept your final manuscript.

Also, be aware that if you are working with hybrid publishers and writers' services, they may charge you extra beyond a certain number of images. For example, you may be allowed up to twenty-five images, but after that you have to pay an extra few dollars per image. These extra charges are often hidden in the fine print of a very long contract, so make sure you know the policy before you decide to insert a hundred illustrations.

Most likely, your interior images will be in black and white. Full-color interiors are more expensive to print. It's fine if that's what you have in mind, just be aware of the additional cost.

All print images, whether photos or illustrations, must be at least 300 dpi (dots per inch). This is the standard for high-resolution print. Most web images are somewhere around 72 dpi, and will look blurry if they're printed on paper. Your publisher will return images to you if they don't meet the industry standards, as described in your contract. So make sure all your graphics are high-resolution. If you start thinking about these details now, you'll save yourself a major headache later.

## Front and Back Matter

Perhaps the most important pages in your whole book are the front and back matter, at least in terms of getting people to take the next step with your business. Front matter includes all the pages that appear before the first chapter; and back matter includes all the pages that appear after the close of your content.

**Front matter might include:**
- Copyright page
- Title page
- Frontispiece (an illustration, usually on the left page, facing the title page)
- HVB page (High-Value Bonus, usually a freebie readers can get from your website)
- Epigraph (a quotation to set the tone of the book)

- Dedication page
- Table of contents
- Foreword
- Preface
- Introduction

**Back matter might include:**
- Epilogue
- Appendix
- Glossary
- Resources
- Bibliography
- Index
- About the author
- Acknowledgements (this could also go in the front)
- Main offer
- Additional products, services, or books

Too many authors ignore these pages and don't get the powerful marketing benefits they can provide. Remember, you are the boss of your book! You can include whatever you want. Certain pages are expected to be there, such as the copyright page, dedication, and table of contents. These help lend credibility if you're self-publishing. They make the book feel more "real".

You've already read how your contents page itself can do the job of selling your book. You've also seen how an HVB can help move people from your book to your website. What about a resources page? This can include affiliate offers or other resources, such as your products and services. You can also mention your brand and products/services on the About the Author page. Much of the front and back matter of your book can be straight-up marketing, and the readers don't mind. In fact, they expect it. If you've done a good job with your book's main content, some readers will naturally want to know where they can get more information from you or how they can hire you.

Don't forget that these extra marketing pages can include illustrations or photographs. If your book is mostly text, a big graphic advertising your offer will draw attention. Take some serious time to design your front and back matter pages. They are some of the most valuable real estate in your whole book.

## Time Management

You're busy, I get it. If you're too busy to write your book, hire a ghostwriter. Or maybe just forget about having a book at all. It's only one of the best tools around for positioning you as an expert and marketing your company. You don't really need one, do you?

You do?

Well then, you'd better have a strategy for finishing the darn thing!

There are few things worse than having a half-done book sitting on your hard drive that never gets published. Time is short. So stop screwing around with your manuscript and get it done already.

Here are a few strategies to keep you moving forward:

**1. If you haven't created your question-based outline yet,**

**go back and do it.** This is the best time management tool you have when it comes to writing your book.

**2. Write every single day.** How? Break it up into little chunks of writing time. Even if you only spend ten minutes answering one question on your outline, that's progress you can be proud of.

If you need some accountability and encouragement, I've set up a daily check-in group on Facebook where you can post your daily writing goals and then come back to let everyone know how successful you were in meeting them. You can find it on Facebook by searching for "writing accountability group".

**3. Write moving forward.** Don't go back and edit your book to death. In fact, you may not want to re-read anything you've written in your draft until it's finished. It's a draft. It's supposed to be a mess! You'll fix everything in the editing stage. Just keep moving forward until you get it done.

**4. Realize your first draft isn't going to be perfect.** It might even suck. That's okay. Keep writing. If it's not written down, you can't fix it.

**5. Set aside a certain time of day for writing, and stick to it.** Maybe you wake up thirty minutes early and write. Maybe you write on your lunch break or evening commute on the train or bus. Pick a time when you're alert and able to think clearly. Write at the same time every day.

**6. Don't set aside a certain time of day for writing.** I know this contradicts what you just read, but some people just need to write when the words come. If the words come for you at different times of the day, that's fine, as long as you're writing every day. Try both ways (a set time, then different times) to figure out which works best for you. And remember, you only have to answer one question at a time. Ten minutes of progress is still progress.

**7. Get the first draft done as quickly as possible,** even if that means skipping over some research you need to do or using placeholder text now and then. It's too easy to start researching something online and then fall down a rabbit hole of distraction. Three hours later, you still don't have the answer you started looking for. I'll often write myself notes to go look something up later. I always put the notes in between brackets <<like this>>. That way, I can just do a global search in my word processing program to find them all and fill them in when I have time.

**8. Don't talk about your book too much as you're writing the first draft.** There's a sort of magical energy surrounding the creation of something that has never existed before. When you talk about it too much, the magic can dissipate. There will be plenty of time for telling people about it later. Right now, focus all your energy into that first draft. If people ask you about it, just tell them it's a secret for now.

**9. Make a commitment and keep it.** A commitment means you're going to do what you say you'll do, no matter what. There's no turning back. There's no Plan B. If you say you're going to write for an hour, or even just 30 minutes, do it! Make your commitments easy to keep at first. Tell yourself you just need to answer one question on the outline, which might only take ten minutes. Once it's done, you've kept your commitment. Then, if you feel like continuing to write, do so. If you don't, it's okay. You've done what you said you'd do.

Think about this. If you have one hundred questions on your outline, and you stick to your commitment to respond to one question a day, you'll be done with your draft in just 100 days. That might seem like a long time to you right now, and that's okay. It's better to work with a commitment you can keep than to set yourself up for failure with a goal that's too lofty or unrealistic.

**10. Create a habit: daisy-chain onto an old habit.** Habits, by definition, are unconscious. They are actions we take without even thinking. We don't plan to go to Starbucks at 3:15 in the afternoon every day. Maybe we did at first, but now it just happens automatically. We don't even have to look at the clock to know it's time. Wouldn't it be nice if writing could become a habit you just do, day in and day out, without thinking about it? It is possible; people do it all the time.

The easiest way to create a new habit is to hook it onto the end of an already existing habit, like linking flowers in a daisy chain. If you'd like to create a morning writing habit, pick a habitual action you already have—like say, making a pot of coffee—and just open up your writing program as soon as you hit the button on the coffeemaker. Or, if you take your dog for a walk first thing every morning, maybe you turn on your computer right after you hang up his leash and take off your coat. Find a physical action, a trigger, which starts the next habit.

Another trick to creating a new habit is to set a ludicrously low threshold for success. Set yourself up to win every single day, and your habit will be reinforced by the positive feedback. What's a ludicrously low threshold? How about opening your computer, and writing only until the coffee is ready. Then you can stop, if you want to. Or only writing 50 new words on the manuscript. Or only writing for six minutes. Set the bar so low that your brain can't logically come up with a reason not to follow through. Most of the time, you'll probably write longer than you set as a minimum. The goal is to create a habit that gets you started. Once you're working, keep on going as long as you can.

Also, celebrate when you succeed. Take a moment to say,

"Yes! I did it! I wrote 50 new words!" There is power in repeated small successes. And before long, you'll be able to stretch your sessions out longer and longer. The success level should always be easily achievable.

Okay, you've got a handle on what you need to do to get your draft written. Remember, it's okay if it's not perfect. One ghostwriter I know calls this stage the Frankendraft because it's often a complete mess! That's fine, as long as you have all the pieces down in rough form. All the questions answered.

Take a deep breath and let out a primal scream . . .

WOO HOOOOOOOO!

You did it!

Celebrate! You've accomplished something millions of people say they want, but never actually do.

Once the celebration is over, you'll be ready to move on to the editing stage.

# CASE STUDY

**The Like Economy:**
**How Businesses Make Money With Facebook**
By Brian Carter

**Author's business:** The Carter Group (digital marketing agency)
**Target market:** Business owners, including entrepreneurs, small businesses, and marketers, who want to expand their marketing onto Facebook in a profitable manner.

**Tell us about your book.**
The Like Economy offers step-by-step techniques and practical lessons drawn from the author's 11 years of experience helping companies double and triple their revenue online. This revenue-focused book is packed with up-to-date ideas and proven solutions with all the details you need to execute crisply, avoid costly mistakes, and reap big profits. Readers learn how to

- Identify your best Facebook profit opportunities.
- Craft Facebook programs that reflect your unique offerings, brands, and customers.
- Use Facebook to supercharge your existing marketing programs.
- Attract super-affordable targeted clicks and fans with Facebook ads.
- Repel negative "brand-bashers".
- Increase visibility.
- Deepen your customer interactions.
- Translate "community" into cash.

**How did you find the writing process?**
It was very intense. It's more work than most people think. It's easier for me than it is for a lot of people, from what they report, but it's still a ton of work. Editing was more work than expected, as well. Getting input from three different types of editors (developmental, copy, and line) was tough. I would usually get upset at the feedback, then settle down, accept it, and make the needed changes.

**Did the book help you achieve your goal?**
I was already successful at attracting clients, getting them results, speaking at conferences, and teaching businesses how to market. However, I was not considered as desirable a speaker as thought leaders who had books. I wanted to reach more people and get paid to speak. The book became an international best-seller, was translated into six languages, and got me into Mashable.com and onto Bloomberg TV. It put me in the higher echelon of author experts. It definitely helped me get paid speaking gigs.

# Chapter Four

## Editing

The first step in the editing stage is to put the manuscript away and do nothing.

Seriously! Let the thing sit for a while, at least two weeks. Your manuscript needs to marinate. All those words need to get to know each other and decide if they like where they're living. Your brain also needs time away from the manuscript. When you sit down to do your second draft, it's important to have fresh eyes.

This doesn't mean you're not working on your book while your manuscript is resting. Keep up your daisy chain habit; you've worked too hard not to keep that going. At this stage, you should be working on marketing content. Maybe you write a few blog posts or set up a social media schedule for the book. Maybe you start writing out a list of potential promotional partners or book reviewers. Keep the time focused on your book, and keep yourself in writing mode. In other words, don't change the habit from writing to checking your email.

After a few weeks have passed, it's time to return to your manuscript and see what you've created. Read through the draft from start to finish with an open mind. You might decide it's the best book ever written, or you might decide it's total crap. Most likely, it's neither of those.

Go through it once without judgment and jot down any notes you want to remember. Your notes might look something like this:

- *I need to add a story to the end of Chapter Two.*
- *The self-esteem exercise on page 35 doesn't make sense, maybe move it to the end of page 48.*
- *I use the word "exceptional" far too often; do a search and find variations.*
- *Fact-check the statistics on page 103.*

Once you've re-read your book, it's time to start your second draft. This is editing you do yourself. The idea here is to get the book as close to perfect as you can. For this edit, you will want to work through the book in order, from start to finish. Don't skip around. Continuity is important now, and you might be surprised to find that you make references to concepts that don't get explained until two chapters later. Or you might find that you use the same example in two different contexts.

The reason you want fresh eyes on this draft is so you can see it the way your reader will: in order. Some books are designed to be read out of order, and that's fine. Just be sure to tell your reader in the beginning whether they can start and stop anywhere, or whether it's important for them to read from start to finish.

Chapter Four

## Keep Moving Forward

This stage can be a slow slog through hell. It's tempting to rewrite and rewrite and rewrite the same paragraph for three weeks and never make any progress. This is a common mistake, so you're not alone if you find yourself over-editing.

The fact is, there are a million ways to say the same thing. If the sentence or paragraph you've written communicates what you're trying to say, rewriting seventeen times is probably a waste of time. Rewrite it a few times, if you must, to make the meaning clear and the sentence structure at least close to traditional. But don't fuss over every single line of your book. Over-editing is a lovely procrastination technique. However, your goal is to get this book finished and out into the world where it can do some good! So, avoid the temptation.

How long does this process take? That depends on how long your book is, how much time you devote to editing, and how well you communicated your message in the first draft. It might take a couple of weeks, or it might take a couple of months. Some people edit their manuscript for years until they just decide to chuck the whole project. Be reasonable. There's no expected timeline here. As long as you're continually moving forward, you will eventually come to the end.

Check yourself weekly. If you started the week editing on page four, and you ended the week on page twenty-seven, you're fine. On the other hand, if you started on page four and end the week on page six, you might want to speed it up a bit.

## What Should You Edit at This Stage?

At this stage, you should edit for meaning and flow, not for perfect grammar and spelling. If you find a mistake, correct it, but that's not what you should pay attention to most at this stage. All the grammar issues will be handled later in the process, ideally by a professional copyeditor or proofreader.

Ask yourself the following questions as you edit:

- Did you say what you meant to say?
- Is your point clear to the reader?
- Do you use jargon they might not understand?
- Do you explain concepts at too high or too low a level for your target audience?
- Could you use some additional examples, exercises, or stories?
- Are you mentioning your products and services too often or trying to sell too aggressively? (Or not enough?)
- Is the word count way too high, indicating you need to make cuts?
- Or do you need to add content (not fluff!) to bulk up the work?

Get through your entire manuscript. Edit away. Make huge cuts, if necessary. Move chapters around so they make more sense. Add chapters, if you need to. Once you have a second draft that makes you happy, it's time to invite feedback from others.

Chapter Four

## When to Hire a Professional Editor

No author should publish a book without having a professional editor look it over. Sometimes you're going to need several editors.

If you plan to publish the book with a traditional New York publisher or an established independent publisher, they might assign you an editor at no cost to you. However, the publisher will take your finished manuscript and hand it over to an in-house editor. This person will scrutinize it through the lens of a professional book creator. They know what's standard in the business, and they will help your book conform to the industry standard as much as possible. This is both good and bad.

You definitely want your book to be what's called "industry standard." You want the pages to look and feel like a "real" book. So your editor is doing you a favor by giving you guidelines to follow.

On the other hand, some editors completely destroy an author's vision and the book's uniqueness. In traditional publishing, the editor works for the publisher. And, in most cases, the publisher has the final say. If they decide your book has to have a red cover and ten chapters of exactly twenty pages each, that's pretty much what you're going to get. They might allow you to negotiate some, and you may even be able to change their minds. However, it's unlikely. This is why it's critical to get the right publisher, if you're planning to go the traditional route. Find a publisher who understands your vision for the book.

If you decide to self-publish, you have the final say over the editing, the design, and the cover. This is great, but it's a double-edged sword. You know your business, but you probably don't know the book business. There are so many nuances an editor will pick out that you probably won't find on your own, like which side of the page to start a new chapter. So, that's when you hire a professional. You outsource your late-stage editing to someone who knows the book industry, and who will work with you to make your vision a reality.

Freelance editors often come from previous jobs at the big publishing houses, so they really know what they're doing. While you still maintain the final word on whether their edits are incorporated into the final book, you'd be wise to listen to these experts and take their advice seriously.

## Structural Editing

There are different types of editing that occur at different stages in the process. The first is a structural or developmental edit. An editor evaluates the manuscript for meaning and flow, just like you did when you created your second draft. They will make suggestions and give you ideas for additional content or maybe recommend you make drastic cuts. If you're working with a book coach, they will often collaborate this editing with you.

Some business people will skip this type of edit if they're *absolutely sure* their manuscript communicates the message effectively and flows well. However, if this is your first book, I recommend you go through this process at least once. You don't know what you don't know, and this feedback can be truly eye-opening.

## Chapter Four

## COPYEDITING

The next kind of edit is a copyedit or line edit. This is where the "red pen" comes out and all the grammar, spelling, punctuation, and formatting mistakes are corrected. Do not skip this edit! I don't care if you got all As in English class, or you had your partner look it over (because they're really smart). Get a professional to do a copyedit.

The fact is, even if you are an excellent writer and your spelling is impeccable, you will still make mistakes. And you will miss them when you read through your manuscript. You can't help it. Your brain automatically fills in missing letters and rearranges sentences so they look correct. It takes a trained eye—one that didn't write the manuscript—to find all the little errors. Every manuscript I send to a copyeditor comes back with mistakes to correct. Every one. Even though I write for a living, I still need a copyeditor to polish my work.

After you get your copyedits back, you need to go through them and decide which ones you agree with and which ones you don't. If you're self-publishing or using a hybrid publisher, you are the boss of your book. So, you have to go through and accept or reject every single edit and suggestion. This is tedious. Take it in stages, maybe work on ten pages at a time and then give it a rest.

Also, don't take the edits personally. This one is hard for a lot of authors. The editor is trying to help you create an exceptional book, one you can be proud of for the rest of your life. It's okay if your spelling isn't perfect; that's why you hired an editor. Thank them for finding the mistakes. Don't beat yourself up over the corrections.

## Beta Readers

Once you've gone through all the copyedits and you have what you believe to be the final manuscript, it's time to ask for some limited feedback from a couple of carefully chosen readers. Pick a few people to be beta readers, and ask them to give you feedback on the book. (You and your editor were the "alpha readers", so these people are the next in line to read your book.) There are certain things you want to consider when selecting beta readers. So, let's go through a few strategies for getting the most out of this stage.

**1. Choose readers who are in your target audience.** While it's flattering to ask your best friend or your mom to read your book and give feedback, they might not be the best people to evaluate your message. You want your beta readers to understand what you're talking about. They should relate to your message. Otherwise you'll get generic feedback like, "It's a nice book, dear." Or, "I didn't really understand it, but it reads well." If you are writing a book for real estate agents, get a few agents to be your beta readers. If you're writing a book for dog groomers, ask some dog groomers for feedback.

**2. Choose a handful of people.** Too much feedback is as bad as too little. If you give your book to twenty-five people, you're going to spend months getting through all the comments. It's a personal decision, though. I like to ask four people; you might want a few more or a few less. I wouldn't go with more than eight, though.

**3. Choose people you can trust to give honest criticism.** Your mom is probably not going to tell you your book sucks. She's going to tell you what you want to hear—that you did a good job or that she's so proud of you. That's great for boosting morale, but it doesn't help you improve your book.

The goal here is to see if people in your target audience get the message you're trying to convey. Do they understand what you're talking about? Are you clear? Do you give enough examples? Do they believe the ideas or concepts you're selling them? Does the book make them want to hire you or visit your store?

You want beta readers who will say things like, "Really? I don't believe this for a second!" (That tells you to add in more supporting evidence.) Or, "I don't understand what you're trying to say here. What's the point?" (That tells you to add in more examples or make the explanation more clear, maybe break it down into steps.)

Make sure you tell your beta readers this is what you're looking for. You don't need them to do another copyedit, unless they find an obvious typo or spelling mistake. (Copyeditors are human, too. Sometimes they miss things.)

**4. Choose people who actually read books, and have time to read this one.** So many people don't read these days. And when they do, it takes them a year to finish one book. You don't want those people as your beta readers! You want people who like to read, who read quickly, and who are willing to take the time to read your book and give you feedback by a deadline.

It's important that you set a deadline, otherwise it's really easy to put off publishing your book until everyone reports in. Give them two weeks, and ask them if they have the time to commit to that deadline. If they don't, find someone else.

**5. Consider giving each beta reader just a portion of the book to read.** If your book is divided into sections, or each chapter can be read independently, you can make life easier on the readers if you just give them a small portion of the book to read. Busy people are more likely to put off reading a whole book. It's easier if they only have to comment on ten or twenty pages.

**6. Give them specific instructions for giving feedback.** It can be difficult for beta readers to know what types of feedback will be useful. So, tell them exactly what you're looking for. Do you want them to make comments directly in the manuscript? Do you want them to type their comments into a Word doc or a spreadsheet? Give them some guidance.

One great way to do this is to have them fill out a questionnaire, answering specific questions. Then, tell them they can always add feedback, if they want to. Some questions might be:

- What was your overall opinion of the book?
- What's one part you really liked?
- What's one part you were confused about?
- What's one thing you wish I had included that wasn't there?
- What questions did you have at the beginning of the book?
- What questions did you have at the end of the book?
- Were there any places you were confused or lost?
- What's one thing you think would improve the book?
- Is there anything else you'd like to add?

By offering feedback on the book, your beta readers will become invested in it. They will feel like they had a hand in creating it, and they can become your biggest allies in the

## Chapter Four

marketing process. The same thing happens when you ask your social media followers or the people on your email list for opinions on your cover design and titles. People like to feel involved.

They also like to feel special, so treat them specially. Thank them by name in your acknowledgments. Give them some special shout-outs on social media. And ask them to give the book an honest review on Amazon after it's been published.

Sometimes you can go through the beta reading process even after the book is published. Tell your chosen readers you're compiling ideas for a second (or third) edition, and you're looking for feedback. Request volunteers from your followers. Don't lie about the second edition just for marketing reasons. But if your book has been around for awhile, the beta reading process can reinvigorate it, and get people excited about it all over again.

After you get comments back from your beta readers, once again you have to make decisions about whether to follow their input. Some suggestions will be pure gold, and others will only make sense to the individual reader. Keep your target market in mind as you make these decisions. You want to find the best way to communicate your message to the most people.

Do not be tempted to rewrite half the book. And you will be tempted. You'll want to keep adding and changing things even after the book is published. At this point in the game, though, small changes for clarification's sake are all you're looking for. Little tweaks.

If the feedback from readers is really extensive, and you really must do a major overhaul, go back and talk to a structural editor. If you skipped that stage, maybe you shouldn't have.

These editors are experts at organizing your content into a readable book. They might be able to help you rearrange the book so it makes more sense. Or they might tell you that your beta readers were a bit overzealous, and the book is fine the way it is. Most likely, the truth lies somewhere in the middle.

## Proofreading

After your book has been finalized, and all the layout and formatting is done, it's time for one final proofread. Do not proofread your own book. This is a job for a professional, preferably one who hasn't been closely involved with the work up to this point. Proofreading combs out any last typos, spelling errors, or formatting mistakes. Proofreaders are looking for mistakes that have nothing to do with how you deliver your message.

Although proofreading sounds purely cosmetic, it's important. Your reputation and credibility are on the line. Mistakes make you look careless, and that's not the image you want for your business. Potential customers could lose respect for a business that is represented by such shoddy writing. If you have a traditional or hybrid publisher, they might take care of this step for you. If you're self-publishing, you should hire a professional proofreader before you upload or send your book off to print.

There's no magic formula for the order of the edits. Some authors skip the structural edit, get beta readers, have a copyeditor look at the grammar, and then publish. Others have beta readers do the first edits, then talk to a structural editor and copyeditor. Some only have a proofreader do a once-over before they go straight to publishing (Note: This is not recommended).

Ultimately, it's up to you and your budget. Editing does cost some money, but a good editor is worth every penny.

## How to Hire an Editor

By this point, you've spent so much time, money, and effort creating your book. Hiring the right editor is a critical step toward a finished book you can be proud of. If you have a publisher, they will assign you an editor. In this case, they know and trust that editor to get the manuscript ready according to their guidelines, not yours.

When you're self- or hybrid-publishing, the whole editing shebang is up to you. And you probably don't have any guidelines to go by. So, it's critical that you find an editor you trust. Here are some tips for finding the right editor for you.

**Get recommendations from other authors:** You probably shouldn't start your search for an editor on Google. That's just asking for a long, drawn-out, frustrating search. Do you know other business people who've written books? Ask them who did their editing. Ask your contacts on LinkedIn. Or ask around in some online forums for professionals in your industry. Referrals are the fastest way to find reliable editors.

**Look for experience in your genre:** Are you writing a book on real estate investing? You probably shouldn't hire a science fiction editor! You want someone who is familiar with the concepts and terminology in your book.

One way to do this is to head to the bookstore and find a

book you think is similar to yours. Then, read through the acknowledgements. Almost always, you'll find the author gives a big shout-out to the editor. Once you have the name, just head to Google and look them up. If you can't find someone who has edited a book just like yours, then at least find someone who works with nonfiction business books.

**Expect positive energy and excitement about your book:** If the editor isn't excited about your book, they're probably not going to give you a good edit. Explain what you want this book to do for you and your business, and see what their reaction is. Are they happy and looking forward to working with you to make it an awesome book? Or will your book just be another in a long line of grammar exercises piling up on their to-do list? You'll be able to feel the energy if it's a good fit.

There are plenty of editors out there! Don't settle for one who isn't right for your book.

**Interview their past clients:** Every editor worth their salt will post at least a few of the books they've edited on their website. Email the authors of those books and ask what their experience was like. Would they recommend this editor?

Reassure them that you won't divulge what they tell you. You want an honest recommendation or warning. And remember, you're a stranger to them. They don't know you and might not trust you. So, approach them with respect and be polite.

**Take a test-drive before you sign a contract:** Request a sample edit of a few pages or a chapter before you sign a contract. Make sure this is an editor who will make great suggestions and be easy to work with.

**Expect on-time delivery:** If the editor misses a deadline on a sample edit, that's a huge red flag. Discuss the timeline up front, and make sure they meet the deadline. Editing does take time, so don't expect an overnight job. However, the last thing you want is for your manuscript to disappear for months with no communication.

## Done For You vs. Done With You Editing

If you know spelling and grammar are your weak points, and you just want to publish a book for marketing purposes, it might make sense to ask your editor to make the changes to the manuscript for you. If you don't know the difference between "affect" and "effect", or couldn't care less about verb tenses, there's not much point in making you decide whether to accept or reject the changes they recommend. Tell them that, if it's a grammar, spelling, or punctuation correction, they should go ahead and just make the change.

On the other hand, if you're planning to write more books, it makes sense to learn basic grammar rules. Strengthen your weak points. If you have a serious issue with writing passive sentences, a good editor can show you how to fix that problem forever.

Talk with your editor and decide together whether you want to see every single edit, or you just want them to make the changes and be done with it. Be aware, though, that you're trusting them to make the right changes. If that's the way you decide to go, make sure you hire a consummate professional. Don't cheap out!

## It's Not the Editor's Job to Write Your Book

Many editors complain that authors come to them with a book that's "almost done." The author thinks it's ready for an editor to take over when, in fact, it's not. Those authors really need to find a ghostwriter or book architect at this stage. Editors only work with finished manuscripts. Don't expect them to do a lot of research or invent whole chapters for you. They are not the creators. Your book is only ready for an editor when you have written the entire manuscript and revised it at least once.

## How Much Do Editors Charge and How Long Does it Take?

Just like hiring a ghostwriter or a book marketer, you can find an editor in just about every price range—from the ridiculously cheap to outrageously expensive. And those words mean different things to different people. You can find editors who charge hourly, anywhere from $15 to over $100 an hour. You can find others who charge by the word, anywhere from 1 to 10 cents per word. Some will give you a flat rate anywhere from several hundred to a few thousand dollars.

The reason a good editor costs more is because they're not just reading the material once and making comments. They crawl through the manuscript at a snail's pace, reading one sentence at a time, scrutinizing every paragraph and every chapter. They look up word spellings and grammar usage as needed. They might create a style sheet for you. They go through your entire manuscript multiple times. The whole process takes time and intense mental energy. Editing is a skilled craft, one that's worth paying for.

Every manuscript is different. Every author needs different things from an editor. So really, it's about your budget and your needs. I tell my authors to expect to pay between one and two thousand dollars for copyediting and proofreading. If they need it finished in less than three weeks or so, they should expect to pay more.

## How to Help Your Editor

If you want a great edit, it helps to turn in the best manuscript you possibly can. Spelling and grammar-check programs are a good start. If you want to pay for a higher level of automated checking, you can use a service like Grammarly (www.grammarly.com).

The problem with these programs is they don't allow for individual expression, colloquialisms, sentence fragments, or your own quirky voice. The programs are automated, so they will point out *every* error. Many of the errors could be intentional, and don't need to be fixed. So, you still have to go through and tell the software to ignore some errors and fix others. Software is not a replacement for a human editor. However, it's a great start for making your manuscript as clean as possible before you give it to your editor.

There will be certain words, sentences, and paragraphs in your manuscript that you know are going to raise red flags with an editor. For example, maybe you want to use British spelling. Or you have a loose, conversational style with lots of sentence fragments. Or your industry uses common words in uncommon ways. Or you intentionally included lots of white space between your paragraphs. Tell your editor about these in advance using a document called a style guide. A detailed style guide makes the editor's life easier, and it makes your life easier.

For example, I ghostwrote a book for a gentleman in the automobile business. In that industry, they call walk-in customers "Ups." As in, "Don't just stand around waiting for an Up." This is clearly an unconventional use of the word, so I told the editor about it in the style guide.

I wrote for another client and he liked to use ellipses a lot . . . Like, a LOT. There was a specific reason for using them, though, and he didn't want them taken out. So, we added that to the style guide.

Another common issue for me is that I use the word "they" as a gender-neutral singular pronoun (instead of saying "he or she" all the time). Some editors are fine with this usage, some aren't. Since I know I want it to stay that way, I put it into the style guide.

The easiest way to create a style guide is to make notes while you're writing your draft. Whenever you come across an unusual word or spelling, or a grammar issue that you know might trip up an editor, write it down. Your editor will appreciate that you took the time to make their job easier. A good editor will also expand the style guide during the editing process to ensure that everyone involved with the book stays consistent.

There's no hard-and-fast rule about how many rounds of editing you'll need. One publisher I work with estimates it takes up to twenty rounds back and forth between her editors and the author before they have a final manuscript. Twenty! So, if this process takes longer than expected, don't fret. Remember that you want to wind up with a book you can be proud of.

Once you've gone through and considered every edit, it's time to move into the publishing stage.

Ready? Let's go!

## CASE STUDY

**Conquer Your Closing:**
**Insider Secrets for Today's Savvy Home Buyer**
By Karen Simpson-Hankins

**Author's business:** KarenSimpsonHankins.com (mortgage expert)
**Target market:** Anyone interested in buying a home in today's complex, overwhelming, and competitive mortgage market

**Tell us about your book.**
I wrote the book to educate consumers about what happened in the mortgage credit crisis and how they can protect themselves and shop for a mortgage like a pro in today's new mortgage market. I was fed up with the way consumers were being treated, and I wanted them to have access to the inside knowledge that banks and lenders don't readily share. The book shows them how to stop taking the first loan that a lender offers and shop for their Right Fit Mortgage® while saving time, money, and stress in the process.

**How did you find the writing process?**
I wrote the book *Conquer Your Closing* and its companion workbook myself, both of which are available on Amazon and on my website. It was the best experience of my life. I learned a lot about who I am and what I am capable of! I learned that I love to write, and completing the book has given me the confidence to pursue other projects. Becoming an author has taken me on adventures that I never thought possible!

**Did the book help you achieve your goal?**

*Conquer Your Closing* (Kindle Edition) went to #1 in several categories on Amazon. It has provided me with many opportunities, such as my own nationally syndicated radio show, Surviving the Credit Crisis, numerous speaking engagements, and other writing projects. It has helped my mortgage career by setting me apart from the other mortgage professionals in my industry. I also received the 2013-2014 National Association of Professional Women's "National VIP Woman of the Year Award" in real estate. I have also just finished the revised edition of *Conquer Your Closing*.

# Chapter Five

# Publishing and Distribution

Okay, at this stage you've written your book. You've edited and polished it until it's darn near perfect. And now it's time for the moment of truth—publishing that sucker!

Here's how publishing used to work for the vast majority of authors. You worked your butt off writing a great manuscript. Maybe you worked for months, or more likely it was years of your life, poured into a stack of 8.5 x 11 inch pages.

Then, you wrote a book proposal and a query letter, and mailed it out to agents and/or publishers you hoped would be interested in your work. Most of the time, you got no response. Sometimes, you would receive a "thanks, but no thanks" letter in the mail months later. A very tiny percentage of fortunate authors would receive a "Please send us the manuscript." letter, or *maybe* a phone call.

If you were one of the lucky few, you packaged the whole manuscript in a special box and mailed it out. Then, you sat around nervously waiting, hoping your work would be worthy. That you would be chosen.

That, just maybe, your work was good enough.

Most of the time, you received a "thanks, but no thanks" letter, and you started the process all over again.

If you were one of the blessed chosen to be published, you embarked on a year-long journey, which *might* have been glorious, or might have been hell. You might have received a little money as an advance against royalties. If your book sold well, you received a small percentage of the profits. If it didn't sell, the publisher took a loss and you received nothing beyond what you were given as an advance. Most books failed.

The publisher held complete control over the book, including the content, cover design, layout, and distribution. And, because the publisher took all the risks and paid all the money to print the book, they also owned some or all of the copyrights and took the lion's share of the profits.

Pretty depressing, huh?

## That Was Then, This is Now

Today, authors have the ability to outsource everything a publisher would do to create a book. Companies have been established to allow anyone to hire out editing, design, typesetting, publishing, and distribution services. Publishing is no longer reserved for the chosen few. Anyone can publish a book.

There are reasons to go with a traditional publisher, sure. Sometimes, traditional publishing actually is the best option. If you really want the name Random House or Wiley or another well-known publisher on the cover of your book, then maybe it makes sense, for the sake of prestige. And you may want someone else to handle all the publishing details so you don't have to.

But there are so many other options now!

There are so many ways to publish your book, it doesn't make sense to hope and pray that a traditional publisher decides to take a chance on you. It doesn't make a lot of sense to sign over your rights to the manuscript, either. No matter how you publish, you will be expected to do most (or all) of the marketing and sales. So, why give away the majority of the profits? You probably know your target audience better than a traditional publisher, and you probably know how to market your book better, too.

In the past, it was a matter of *whether* your book would be published.

Screw that! Today, it's a matter of *how* you will publish.

Let's look at what a publisher actually does to produce your book. Then, let's go over the various options you have, so you can make an informed decision about how you want to publish your book.

## What Exactly Does a Publisher Do?

There's a great mystery surrounding what a publisher actually does to turn that stack of paper or electronic document into an actual book. The fact is they do a lot of work. However, each piece of the book-creation puzzle can either be handled by you, or outsourced to a professional. Often, you can outsource to the same professionals who are currently working for the publishers. How crazy is that?

Does it cost you to publish? Yes! Either in money, or in time and energy.

Is it worth it? Absolutely!

Here's what has to happen to make your book a reality:

**Editing:** We've already discussed editing pretty thoroughly. It's a huge process. And it's one that can be outsourced based on your budget.

**Interior layout, design, and formatting:** How does the inside of your book look? Interior layout and design takes care of the fonts and page numbering and margins and all the stuff that needs to be formatted inside the front and back covers. This can also be outsourced.

**Cover wrap design:** Not only do you need a professionally-designed front cover, but also a full cover wrap. The wrap includes the front and back covers and the spine. It's important that the whole package for your book looks professional. This can be outsourced as well.

**Pricing, page count, and book size:** These are decisions you need to make based on the industry standard for your genre. You don't need to figure this out yourself. You can either spend time doing the research, or you can spend money to get expert advice on what's best for your book.

**ISBN and bar codes:** ISBN stands for International Standard Book Number, and it's how books are identified. A bar code is a visual representation of the ISBN and price of your book. If you plan to sell your book through retail or online outlets, you need to have both. You get them online from Bowker at www.MyIdentifiers.com. If you plan to have a print version, ebook, and audiobook, you will need three different ISBNs. You can purchase these yourself for about $150. Or, you can save money

## Chapter Five

by purchasing in bulk, if you need more than one. These items need to be on the back cover, so make sure you get them before you finalize your cover wrap. Also, you'll need to know the price of your book before you purchase your bar code.

**Printing:** Once the book is fully designed and ready to go, it needs to be printed. There are loads of places to get your book printed in batches, or one at a time (known as POD, or print-on-demand). Companies like 48HourBooks.com specialize in batch printing books. The larger the batch, the less money you pay. If you don't want to store boxes of books in your garage, you might decide POD is a better way to go. POD companies like CreateSpace and Lightning Source print and ship your books one at a time as needed.

**Distribution:** This is a big piece of the puzzle. Distribution means how you plan to get your book out to people. Many business authors don't really care about bookstore distribution. They don't need to be in every Barnes & Noble or Chapters bookstore. For them, it's enough to be sold online with Amazon, Barnes & Noble and other retailers.

You could also distribute your book on your company website, or in person at speaking events. You could have corporate sponsors or industry associations distribute it for you. There are so many ways to sell your book! Guess what? This can be outsourced, too.

If you want to see your book in bookstores, you're probably going to need to hire a distributor or go the traditional publishing route. If you want to learn more about how distribution works, I strongly recommend you go to www.NewShelvesDistribution.com and check out Amy Collins' educational posts and videos.

## Here's a Dirty Little Secret About Publishing

Publishers outsource, too. That's right. Increasingly, publishers are reducing their in-house staff to save money. So, they have to outsource the work. Guess what? You can do the same thing, and keep the profits.

Now, don't get me wrong. It can cost up to $10,000 or $15,000 to outsource, produce, distribute, and market a professional quality book. That's a lot of up-front cost. Traditional publishers put up the money for you. They are taking all the risk that your book will pay off for them. It's a gamble. They hope your book will make enough to pay for the production and also bring in a profit. They take the risk; they get most of the profits. If you don't want to front the money yourself, traditional publishing might be the best way to go.

However, if you have the means to do all the outsourcing yourself, why not just do it and keep the majority of the proceeds?

It used to be that you could spot a self-published book a mile away. But that's not the case anymore. You can completely outsource the production, printing, and distribution and get a top-quality product. It just comes down to money and time. If you have enough of both to invest, I recommend you do so.

## A Word About Profits

At this point, many authors start seeing dollar signs popping up all over the place. So, I feel it's important to tell you that the odds of you making a lot of money on your book are extremely low.

The vast majority of books only sell a couple hundred copies, even if the authors are working hard on marketing. However, the goal with a business book like yours is not to make a ton of money on sales. In fact, sometimes the best thing you can do is give the book away.

Remember the planning stage? You set a goal to sell products or services on the back end. That's where you make your money. And, even if you only sell a few copies of your book, you can get a huge return on your investment.

For example, if you're a speaker and your keynotes go for $5000 (a relatively modest fee), you only need two or three gigs to cover the cost of publishing the book. And, if you do a good job with the book, it could open doors to dozens or hundreds of gigs over the years.

You aren't writing the Great American Novel here. You're using a book format to sell an idea, a system, a methodology—something that ties back to your business. The book is a calling card. It's a door-opener. It's a pre-selling machine. So, don't stress out over how many books you need to sell to break even on the cost of publishing. Think bigger.

## The Pros and Cons of Different Publishing Models

Now that you know what happens during the publishing process, you're better prepared to make a decision about how your book will be published. Not too long ago, the question was *whether* your work would be published. Fortunately, these days it's just a matter of which path you choose to take.

I'm not going to go into the nitty-gritty details about how

to get published along each path. That's a whole 'nother book. There are plenty of reliable resources that give you detailed action plans. Instead, I want to briefly go through the pros and cons of each type of publishing, so you can decide which one might work best for you.

## TRADITIONAL PUBLISHING

We've already covered this one pretty thoroughly. This is what most people think of when they think of publishing. You send a query letter and book proposal to an agent who handles your type of book. If they're intrigued by your letter, they will ask you to send a manuscript. If your manuscript is good enough, they will represent you to the larger publishing houses and try to get you a contract with one of them.

**Pros:** Traditional publishing might be right for you if you have limited funds to invest in self-publishing. These companies have in-house editors and designers, and they take care of the printing and distribution. They will get you into the bookstores and aligned with online retailers like Amazon. The marketing is left up to you. The publisher's name will appear on your book. That's important to many authors.

**Cons:** First of all, the odds that you're going to land a traditional publisher are stacked against you. The only way a publisher is going to take a risk on you is if you can pretty much guarantee your book will sell at least 10,000 copies. If you have a huge mailing list, an active social media following, or some other large platform, you have a much better chance of getting a contract. You will need to write a formal book proposal complete with a summary of your book, marketing data, competitive research, marketing plan, and sample chapters. Your job in the proposal is to prove to the publisher that you have a good idea and you know exactly how you will sell enough copies to make them a profit.

The next strike against traditional publishing is timing. These companies have run the same way for over a hundred years. They move slowly. If you need or want your book published sooner than twelve to eighteen months out, this is probably not a good option for you. They can fast-track certain titles, but unless you're a celebrity or a hot politician, it's unlikely they will bother.

The next problem is control. Many business people enter into publishing agreements under the misconception that they are in charge of their own books. This is not the case. The publisher is in charge. Technically, it's the publisher's book, especially if you signed away too many rights. The publisher decides on the final words that appear in the manuscript, the cover design, the artwork, everything.

I have heard horror stories about authors who signed unfair contracts without realizing the consequences. In one case, a doctor who published his life's work with a New York publisher can't even buy or sell his own book anymore because it's out of print and he doesn't own the rights to it. He runs workshops and has people asking for his book all the time, but he can't give it to them. There are no more existing copies, and he doesn't have the legal right to make more. It's tragic.

Even if you're fine with all of the above, realize that you are still responsible for all the marketing and sales of your book. They will help you get the book into bookstores, sure. But then you have about two weeks to sell a ton of those books before the retailers start returning them for a refund. You have two weeks to impress the bookstores with your sales, and then you have to keep on impressing them or they'll stop stocking your book.

Let's talk about the money for a moment. The publisher takes all the risk, they put up the funds to make the book a reality. So, they also take the lion's share of the profits, if there are any. Most books never earn out their advance, so authors don't see a dime in royalties. This may not matter, since you planned your book to profit on the back end. However, if your book has mass appeal and does manage to sell tens of thousands of copies, you could lose a significant amount of money to the publisher.

If you feel this model is right for you, great! However, I suggest you read through the rest of this chapter so you can get an idea for what else is out there.

## INDEPENDENT (INDIE) PUBLISHING

These publishers are smaller versions of the larger publishers. They offer many of the same services, but they have their own independent business models. You don't usually need an agent to reach these publishers. Often, you can simply research them online and submit a full or partial manuscript by email. It's important that you determine which indie publisher might be right for your book. Each company specializes in different types of books. It's also important that you follow their submission guidelines carefully.

**Pros:** Just like traditional publishers, these companies will assume the financial risk involved in editing, designing, printing, and distributing the book. They will get you into bookstores and partnered with online retailers. You will have some control over the design of your book. And these publishers generally move faster, so you may be able to get your book printed sooner.

**Cons:** Because they are taking on the risk of publishing, they are also going to take a larger share of the profits. Usually, their cut is smaller than it would be if you went with a large traditional publisher. They may not have as large a distribution network, so you may not end up in as many bookstores. (Then again, you might; ask them about their distribution.)

Again, you are going to bear the marketing and sales responsibilities. Some indie publishers are willing to help you get the word out, but you should plan on doing the vast majority of the marketing yourself.

## Self-Publishing

With this model, you publish your own book. Outsource everything the publishers do (or learn to do it yourself) and keep all the profits. Simple, right? Well, sort of.

**Pros:** You keep total control over the entire process, which is great, except for the fact that you also have to keep running your business. Publishing is a huge process, with lots of moving parts. You'll need to be a good project manager to keep everything moving forward.

Since you pay for all the outsourcing, you also get to keep most of the profits from sales. This is only fair, right?

**Cons:** It's common to publish a sub-par book because you don't have professional guidance along the way. When it comes to cover design and interior layouts, so many self-published authors just go with what they like. They don't think about whether their books look professionally published. The reading public has become used to the idea that books that look self-published also tend to read that way. For this reason, most bookstores won't sell self-published books. The term "self-published" is viewed in a negative light because for years it was the same as saying "low-quality". And bookstores only want high-quality books to sell.

Another problem is that bookstores order their stock through distributors. And until recently, self-publishers did not have access to them. This is slowly changing, though, and there are ways around the problem. We'll dive deeper into distribution options later in this chapter.

Here's how to get around the negative "self-published" label: If you publish using CreateSpace or a vanity publisher like Author House, Balboa, or any other publisher where you use an ISBN *they* provide, then you are a self-published author. However…if you buy your *own* ISBN through Bowker at www.MyIdentifiers.com and give yourself a publishing name (such as Tri-Magic Publishing), you have created your own independent publishing house and are now considered "indie-published" instead of "self-published." Another term for creating your own indie company is "author/publisher". When you're an author/publisher, you are technically self-published, but you're creating your own independent publishing company to do it.

Guess what? Bookstores are fine with stocking indie titles. Now, you still have to go through normal distribution channels or the bookstores won't know your book exists. We'll go through that shortly.

You can still use CreateSpace or Lightning Source to do all the POD work, but use *your own* ISBN and publisher name. That way you are technically indie-published, not self-published, and you maintain full rights and control of your book.

## Hybrid Publishing

This is the best of both worlds for business people who want to publish books that build their businesses. In this model, you are sharing the publishing costs with the publisher, and sharing the profits more equally. Usually, you will pay the publisher several thousand dollars, and they take care of details like the interior design and layout, the cover design, the printing, and some of the distribution.

In return, you get a much higher percentage of the profits and you can order your books at wholesale cost, sell them on your own, and keep all the profits. Some hybrid publishers also offer marketing and PR services for an additional fee.

**Pros:** You get a seasoned professional to guide you through the entire process. Anytime you have a question, you have someone to call. This is so valuable! It saves you from untold amounts of wasted time. Hybrid publishers understand the needs of entrepreneurs, speakers, and other business people, so they tend to work faster than other publishers.

You also retain control over the content and design of the book. They will help guide you toward a more professional looking cover, and they may make suggestions on the content. But for the most part, you have a lot of say about how your finished book looks.

You also get distribution to bookstores and online retailers.

This is huge. The hybrid publisher has its own distribution network and can get you access to sales outlets you probably couldn't reach on your own.

**Cons:** It's not cheap. You are partnering with your publisher and sharing the cost to produce the book, so expect to pay at least $2000. If you want additional marketing and PR services, it's going to cost a lot more. Some hybrid publishers charge up to $25,000 for complete done-for-you publishing, distribution, and marketing services. Depending on your book and your back end, it might be a pittance compared to the return you can make on the investment.

The marketing job is still yours. There's no way around it—you have to market and sell your own books. Even if you have great distribution and you're in every bookstore, if you don't make enough sales quickly, the bookstores will return your books for a refund.

So, those are the publishing options you have to choose from: traditional, indie, self-published, and hybrid. The choice really comes down to how much capital you have to invest in the project, timing, and how much control you want over the final product.

## Distribution Basics

How do you get your printed book out into the world? That's distribution. And just like publishing, it's been kept a secret by the big publishers for a long time. These days, though, you can get great distribution for your book, if you know how. The key is knowing which distribution avenues will be most beneficial for your book. Business books are different, and you may have more distribution options than you realize.

Chapter Five

## What is Distribution?

Where are readers going to find your book? The answer used to be simple--bookstores. Fortunately, that's not the case anymore. There are still bricks-and-mortar bookstores, and there are online bookstores. But there are also dozens of other places to distribute your books, including your website, niche websites, in person at your speaking gigs, through industry associations and newsletters, even in gift shops and cafés. Your distribution opportunities are really only limited by your imagination.

## Bookstore Distribution

The place most authors get tripped up is with bookstores. They think they must have their books in Barnes & Noble or Chapters or Books-a-Million. They think they need to have their books on Amazon. (Okay, I'll give you that one. You definitely want your book on Amazon.) So, the big question is how in the world do you get your book into bookstores?

Before we answer that question, let's back up a bit.

Remember way back in the planning stage? What were your goals? What did you want to happen after readers finish your book? Did you want them to:

- Go to your website and sign up for your mailing list?
- Visit your local retail store?
- Hire you as a consultant?
- Hire you to speak at their next conference?

Consider for a moment that you might not need to be in

bookstores to achieve those goals. Here are a few little-known facts about traditional retail bookstores.

- They only order books from known distributors. (You have to get into their catalogs.)
- They demand a steep discount. (You have to sell wholesale.)
- They charge publishers for premium displays. (You have to pay to be on a front table or to have your cover placed face out.)
- They only want books they know they can sell. (You have to fit within their narrow estimate of what people will buy.)
- They will return unsold books for a refund within a short period of time. (You have about two weeks to sell some books, or you're done.)
- They will judge your book by its cover, literally. (You have to create a professional, industry-standard book.)

I don't want you to think you can't or shouldn't get your book into bookstores. I just want you to think about whether that's the best use of your time and money. Retailers have limited shelf space, and very narrow margins. They need to be sure your book is going to make them money. If you think all big chain retailers look the same, there's a reason for that: they know what their customers will buy. Think long and hard about whether your book fits into that scenario.

- Here are some things to consider.
- Does your target audience frequent bookstores?

- Do they frequent the section your book would be featured in?
- Do they buy printed books? Or do they prefer ebooks or audio books?
- Is your book up to industry standards, including features such as size, price, word count, and cover design?
- Does your front cover look professional and similar to other books in your section?
- Will you still make a little money at your price point even after the standard discount?

If you answered *Yes* to these questions, and you're determined to get your book into bookstores, cool! I hope to see your title there. (I am living proof that some people do go to bookstores and browse through the business section looking for interesting books to buy.)

You're going to need a distributor. These companies gather up all the best new books coming out in a particular season and put them into a catalog. The retail stores order books from the distributor's catalogs, sometimes with the help of distributor sales reps. This is the traditional distribution model for bookstores. There are dozens of major distributors, and many have their own programs for author/publishers to get into their catalogs.

For example, one of the largest bookstore distributors is Ingram. They distribute to over 38,000 retailers, libraries, schools and other partners in nearly 200 countries. Until recently, only professional publishers could get into their catalog. Now, you can use their POD service, IngramSpark, and automatically gain access to their distribution network.

You can find a link to a list of distributors and their contact information on the resources page of my website (www.TheProfitableBusinessAuthor.com/resources)

If your book is traditionally published, your publisher will take care of putting your book into their distribution network. If you're indie publishing, you should find out about your publisher's distribution or get help from someone like Amy Collins at New Shelves Distribution. She's been in the book business a long time, and has relationships with all the distributors. She represents authors and helps them get the distribution they need. Not just in the big bookstores, but also in places like Walmart, Costco, and Target. As I mentioned earlier, if your book is truly self-published, bookstores are probably out of the picture.

## Online Retailers

Okay, enough about bricks-and-mortar bookstores. What about all the online retailers like Amazon.com, BarnesandNobleinc.com, and Chapters.com? Since there's no risk to a retailer to stock your book online, it's much easier to put your book up for sale in these places. Often, all you have to do is upload a digital file.

One of the challenges with online retailers is that there are so many. Some offer print books, some offer ebooks, most offer both. That's a lot of uploading! Working out a strategy is important.

For ebook distribution, you can use a service like Smashwords.com to upload once and receive global distribution to all the major ebook retailers, including iBooks, Kobo, Barnes & Noble,

OverDrive, Scribd, Oyster, Baker & Taylor, and Axis 360 (for libraries).

For print distribution online, you'll either need to warehouse hundreds of copies around the country or around the world, or go with print-on-demand (POD). For obvious reasons, POD makes a lot of sense. No books are printed until they are ordered, so there's no wasted print costs and no books to store. Services like CreateSpace and IngramSpark can help you get your book set up as a POD title. (These are the two biggest services, and all other POD companies wind up printing through these two anyway.)

Here's where POD can get tricky. Which service should you use—CreateSpace or IngramSpark? Depending on where you want your books sold, the answer might be both. CreateSpace is directly linked to Amazon. They do a great job with POD books that are ordered through Amazon. However, retail bookstores tend to view Amazon as "the enemy" and don't order through CreateSpace. They order through Ingram. So, if you want your book to have the best chance of getting picked up by bookstores and libraries, you'll want to use IngramSpark for your POD services. If you want a presence in both Amazon and retail bookstores, it's a good idea to set up POD with both companies.

One big issue you need to look out for with online distribution is formatting. When you upload a book for distribution, there's no human to look at it and make sure the pages look correct on a Kindle, Nook, or iBook. It's all done by machine. Ebooks are especially delicate beasts when it comes to formatting. And just because your book looks great on Kindle, doesn't mean it looks the same on a Nook. Be sure to proof all your final versions.

Every online distributor has detailed guidelines to help your book shine on their sales platform. Make sure you follow all the guidelines of the individual companies you distribute through. Or consider hiring an expert to format the manuscript and upload it for you.

## Bypass Distribution and Special Sales

Just like the publishing world is wide open now, the distribution opportunities have never been greater. Start thinking outside the traditional bookstore distribution model. It's not set up in your favor, anyway. Distribution's goal is to get your book in front of your target audience, wherever they are. And it's not necessarily the best idea to put your book into a bookstore next to a thousand other books.

Bypass marketing (or "special sales") is a concept recommended by Jack Canfield, creator of the *Chicken Soup for the Soul* series of books. The idea is that you bypass the bookstores, and find your target audience in other places. Where are your people? Where do they eat? Where do they shop? How can you get your book in front of them, in places where there aren't a lot of other books competing for attention?

You know how distracted you get when you surf online? Maybe you go to Facebook, and then you'll see a video pop up so you click over to YouTube, and then maybe you see an ad on the video so you click that and go someplace else—it's like a never-ending rabbit hole. Well, bookstores can be like that, too. If your book is shelved next to a hundred other books in the same topic area, a reader might come in to buy your book and get distracted. They might walk out of that store with a different book, or with no books at all. You're in direct competition with every other book in that store.

Bypass marketing helps you avoid that problem by distributing books in places like ski areas and national parks, restaurants and bakeries, bridal shops and pet stores—anyplace it makes sense. If you have a book about dog grooming, you might want to put your book into pet stores or maybe even a local grocery store in the pet food aisle. If you have a book about your region's local cuisine, it might make sense to sell it in local tourist destinations and restaurants (especially if you mention the name of the restaurant in the book). If you write a book about bicycle maintenance, you might want to put it into sporting goods stores.

Do you see how this works? Put your books wherever it makes sense. That might be in bookstores and online and in local gift shops. The more places people see your book, the better your chances of selling it.

Don't assume people will go out of their way to look for your book. The odds are stacked against you. If your target readers don't normally go to bookstores, why do you want your book there so badly? Those people are not going to change their habits and drive out of their way to go to a bookstore just to buy your book. They *might* look it up on Amazon and buy it there. But you have a better chance of attracting attention if your book stands out, away from the competition. For example, if you're a speaker, readers might be more inclined to purchase your book at the back of the room.

Think about how you can show up in front of your target audience during their normal activities. For example, if you've written a book for small business owners, where do they usually hang out? They go to Office Depot and Staples, they go to industry conferences, they belong to associations, they talk on small business forums, they attend local networking meetings. How can you get your book in those places?

Another big benefit to distributing your book this way is you can often negotiate a no-returns clause into your sale. When you sell to bookstores, you have to offer a deep discount and the store has the option to return the unsold books for refunds. But with special sales, the association or company buys the books outright. They still get a wholesale discount, but they don't have the option to return unsold books.

I find most business owners know exactly where their customers are, and they have an easy time figuring out where to distribute their books. Usually, it's on the company website, through an association, with online retailers like Amazon, and at speaking events. When you're making your distribution plan in your workbook, write down the obvious places, then think up three or more not-so-obvious outlets.

Don't wait until your book is published before you start making a distribution plan. Start thinking about it as early as possible. Make a list and think outside the box. While you're out running errands, notice places that might consider carrying your book and write them down. It's a good idea to go into those places and create relationships with the owners before you ask them to stock your book. Buy something from them. Show your face from time to time. Support *them* first. Then, when your book comes out, they are much more likely to say "Yes" to selling it for you. This is especially true of local bookstores.

Bypass marketing requires some extra effort on your part,

but it's worth it. Every place you want your book to be sold will require a different path. Establishing relationships with potential sellers and serving them first is a great way to go.

Since marketing is your responsibility no matter which publishing or distribution method you choose, it's critical that you understand how to get the word out about your book. The good news is that marketing a book is just like marketing anything else. And since you're a businessperson, chances are this will all be very familiar to you.

Let's dive into the marketing process next.

# CASE STUDY

**B2B Technology Marketing**
By Hugh Taylor

**Author's business:** Taylor Communications, HughTaylor.com (consulting)
**Target market:** Technology product managers and entrepreneurs

**Tell us about your book.**
Marketing technology products to business customers is a distinct discipline. It doesn't resemble consumer-facing tech marketing at all. It's not even the same as business-to-business (B2B) marketing in general. B2B technology marketing requires a completely different way of thinking about customers, products, and markets, mostly because these factors are in a permanent state of flux.

This book takes a pragmatic, strategically informed view of B2B technology marketing, exploring the essential responsibilities of the executive, including:

- Lead generation
- Sales pipeline
- Strategic messaging
- Supporting the sales team
- Communications and public relations
- Customer preference
- Product marketing

## Chapter Five

**How did you find the writing process?**
I wrote this as a series of blog posts that I compiled into book form. I am a professional writer, so the process was not all that difficult. I did find it quite helpful to work with a professional copy editor to smooth it out and get it ready for publication.

**Did the book help you achieve your goal?**
I wrote the book partly as a way to share my knowledge about B2B technology marketing, a very specialized practice, with product managers and entrepreneurs who may want to know more about it. At the same time, I felt the book would be a good calling card and professional endorsement of my skills as a marketing consultant and content creator. I have found the book to be useful. It establishes a certain level of credibility for me. It also helps encapsulate a discussion that I have had many times over the years, which is that marketing for tech products is quite different from traditional consumer marketing. The book helps me make that point.

# Chapter Six

## Marketing

Congratulations! By this point, you've written, edited, and published your book (or at least, you know *how* you plan to publish your book). That's an accomplishment to be proud of.
    Take a moment and let it all sink in.
    PHEW!

.

.

.

.

    All done?
    Now the real work begins.
    Becoming an author is all about writing and publishing. Becoming a *successful* author—whatever that means to you—is all about marketing. Seriously, marketing is at least 80% of the job. For most fiction authors and people trying to make a living by selling their books, it's a long hard slog. Many of them never do wrap their heads around how to sell a book.

Fortunately, that's won't be you. You have an advantage that many professional authors don't. Business people make great authors because they already understand marketing concepts. There's a good chance you already have a large email list. You understand the value of partnering with other people and leveraging their lists. You may already know how to run paid advertising on Google and Facebook, or at least you know the theory behind it.

Even if you don't know any of this, if you're in business, you know how to get customers. You know what your customers like and don't like, and you know where they gather. I won't promise you that marketing your book will be a piece of cake, but it will certainly be easier than if you knew nothing at all about your business.

## Book Marketing Basics

Since you're in business, you probably already know a lot about marketing. You know how to get your products and services out there. Book marketing is no different. Your book is simply another product you offer.

Unlike many authors trying to make a living off of royalties, you know the real opportunity is using your book to sell your other products and services. So, your marketing efforts will be a little different. You may not need to do anything beyond posting the book on your website with a link to Amazon, and adding it to your email newsletter. Just that little bit of marketing might bring you all the new business you need. Or maybe you need to partner with someone who has a large list and send an email out to *their* audience, giving the book away as a free bonus.

## Chapter Six

Whether you decide to sell your book, give it away, or do something in between, the ultimate goal of marketing is to let as many of the *right people* as possible know that the book is out there and entice them to read it. So, let's review some great ways to get your book in front of lots of targeted eyeballs.

You don't have to do everything listed here. With the exception of a website and email marketing, it's okay to pick and choose which activities work within your schedule and budget. There is no magic formula or series of steps to book marketing. It all works, as long as you do it. Consistency is the key.

## 1. WEBSITE

You must have a presence on the web, a place to send people who are interested in learning more about you, your book, or your business. Your website is your home base. No matter what kind of marketing you're working on, the end goal is to steer people to your website.

If you already have a business website, you might just want to add a special page for your book. Or you might decide the book needs its own website. Either way is fine. If you go for a separate book site, make sure you also feature your book prominently on your main business site. You are an author; people need to know about it.

If you've never created a website before, you might be feeling a little hesitant. Many authors are worried they'll have to learn how to code or that it will cost thousands of dollars to have someone else build their sites. Neither of these scenarios is true. Website technology has evolved to the point where you can build a website in just a few hours, using drag-and-drop tools. You might want to check out services like Wix, Weebly, WordPress, or LeadPages to get started.

The hardest part of building a website is figuring out what to put on it. How many pages do you need? What text do you need to add? The design of your website is entirely up to you, and that's the problem. There are too many options, and it can be paralyzing. Let me give you a hand.

Here are some features you absolutely need to have on your book website.

**Home page:** This is where you feature your book. Give people a little tease. Tell them about the book, and why they should buy it. You might include a video book trailer, or some reviews and testimonials. Be sure to include all the places people can buy your book, including links where appropriate.

**About the author:** People are going to want to know about you. What's your background? What qualifies you to write this book? What are your hopes and dreams for people who read the book? Be sure to include a picture of yourself (one with a little personality, please). You might even consider creating a video for this page. Videos help people feel like they know you, and that's part of the "know, like, trust" equation for sales.

**Content page:** This can be a blog, a podcast, or a series of articles or videos. It's content you create that's relevant to the book. This content gives you a reason to post on social media and email people. Instead of trying to figure out what to say in this week's email newsletter, you can just say, "Hey! Check out this article on Five Ways to Improve Your Leadership Skills" and then link back to this content page on your website. Content marketing is one of the best ways to help people get to know, like, and trust you—and to buy your book!

**Email opt-in form:** One of your primary jobs as an author and a businessperson is to build your email list. To do that, you need to have a way to collect email addresses. On every page of your website, near the top somewhere, include a form that encourages people to sign up. It's a good idea to give them something in return for subscribing, a "thank you" gift of sorts. Maybe it's a recorded webinar, a PDF report, or a video tutorial. It doesn't matter what you offer, as long as it's something people want and is relevant to your book and your business.

**Contact information:** Add your contact information to every page of your website. It can be just an email address, or you can include a physical address and phone number. It's important that journalists and reviewers can get in touch with you easily. Don't make them hunt for the information, they may not bother.

**Media page:** You're going to be reaching out to the media frequently—journalists, bloggers, podcasters and other media professionals all have the power to publicize your book for free. A news story beats the hell out of an expensive ad that people will most likely ignore anyway. You want to make their jobs brain-dead easy by giving them everything they need to publish a story about you and your book right on your website. In the old days, this was a physical media kit that you sent out to journalists. Today, you simply put all the materials on a media page on your site.

Your media page should include

- An author bio in several lengths—two sentences, 50 words, 200 words, 400 words
- A book synopsis in several lengths—short, medium, long

- Author and book photos—both low resolution and high resolution for print
- A press release—base this on the problem your book solves
- A tip sheet—gives journalists some quick tips to print
- Contact information—email, office phone number, and maybe a physical address
- Sample interview questions—broadcasters love these!
- Speaker's one sheet—all the vital information about your speaking on one page
- Testimonials and reviews of the book—update these often.
- Purchase information—where can people buy your book?
- Review copy information—how can reviewers get a copy for free?

That's it, that's all you need to have on your website. In fact, you can put all this information on a single page, if you want to. Don't make it more complicated than it has to be. Get a basic site up with this information on it. You can always go back and add or change things later. Your website is critical. Don't get overwhelmed or let intimidation stop you from just getting it done!

## 2. Email Marketing

Once again, if you're already running your business, you probably already do a fair amount of email marketing. If you're brand new to it, here's how it works. An interested reader goes to your website and signs up for your list. Maybe they've already bought your book, or maybe they are just checking you out. Either way, once they're on your list, they will receive a series of automated email messages (called autoresponders) for a few days or weeks.

The frequency is up to you, but you want readers to get used to seeing you in their inbox. After the automated messages have all been sent, you can send weekly or bi-weekly "newsletters" to keep them engaged with you and your brand. The newsletter-style emails are called broadcast emails.

The biggest question I get about email marketing is, "What should I say in my emails?" This is where having a regular content plan is helpful. If you blog regularly, or you have a podcast or YouTube channel, every time you put out a new piece of content, you can send an email letting people know about it and linking over to the content. You can certainly let people know about your products and services in the email. After all, the ultimate goal is to attract and retain customers.

Just don't be obnoxious with the selling. Remember that the people on your list have given you permission to market to them, but they can always click the unsubscribe button and revoke that permission.

### 3. Social Media Marketing

Many people will tell you that social media marketing is critical to your success. Others will tell you it's a complete waste of time. Both groups are right, because every individual has his or her own unique experience with social media. I know business authors who use nothing but Facebook ads and sell plenty of books. I also know authors who spend all day bouncing back and forth from social site to social site and never get any traction. The key is in the word *social*. Social media is all about being social.

When you go out to a cocktail party or networking event, do you walk up to someone and immediately start pitching your product? Of course not.

Would you ever go out on a blind date and ask the person to marry you in the first five minutes? Not likely.

Yet that's exactly what you're doing when you respond to a new follower on Twitter with "Thanks for following. Here's a link to my book!" Dude, I don't even know you. Don't push your stuff on me.

The appropriate response is "Thanks for following. It's nice to meet you." Or maybe you ask them a question based on some information in their profile, "How's the weather up there in Maine?" Be social on social media. Use your profile to encourage curiosity about your business and your book. You can post about your book, sure. Just don't do it too often, and don't be obnoxious about it.

A couple of other questions I get are "Which social media platform is the best?" and "Do I have to be on all of them?" The answers might surprise you.

The best social media platform for you is wherever most of your readers are. Is your target audience young? They're probably not on Facebook; instead, try Instagram. Is your target audience primarily women? Then Pinterest would be a great choice for you. Are you trying to reach people over 35? Facebook, baby! That's not to say there aren't teenagers on Facebook, or men on Pinterest. It's just that each platform has a primary demographic. And if you're trying to decide which is the best platform for you—pay attention to the demographics.

You do need to have a *presence* on all the major social media platforms, including Facebook, Twitter, Instagram, Pinterest, and LinkedIn. But all that means is you set up a detailed profile, add in some information about your book and your business, and tell people the best place to connect with you. You might say something like, "Thanks for finding me on Facebook. I am most active over on Twitter. Please join the party over there." Add in some information about where they can buy your book. Then forget about it! Focus your attention on interacting with and serving the people on the one (or maybe two) social platforms you like best.

### 4. Online Marketing

There are about a jillion ways to market your book and your business online, and it's really easy to get caught up in all the latest strategies and tactics. It's so easy, in fact, that you can wind up researching yourself right out of business! Internet marketing is a massive topic full of experts waiting to sell you their latest solution. Some experts are mind-blowingly smart, others are completely unethical scammers. Who do you trust? What's "really working" to sell books right now?

The biggest problem with online marketing is that it's always changing. There's always a faster, cheaper way to get traffic (people) to your website. There's always a newer, better way to get conversions (sales). You've got paid search and organic search. There's search engine optimization (SEO) for Google, YouTube, Amazon (and every other search engine out there). You've got content marketing in all its glorious forms (blogging, podcasting, video marketing), as well as guest content creation. All that content can be syndicated, of course. The new cool kid on the block is retargeting. And what about social media? That ties into the online stuff somehow. And this list only scratches the surface of what's possible.

I've spent a decade learning most of these methods, and implementing some. And I can tell you it all comes down to knowing the basics, just like everything in life. If you understand the foundations of marketing, you can pick and choose which of the latest strategies is right for you. The absolute best book I've read on this topic is *DotComSecrets* by Russell Brunson. It teaches the foundations, as well as some cool new tactics.

Let me break it down for you. Online marketing means getting the word out about your book on the Internet, right? Behind all the technology are the *people*. At the end of the day, you need to reach *people*.

And people are funny. They don't like to be sold, but they love to buy. They don't like being talked at, but they love conversations. They're smart enough to figure out how to find your book, if they're interested. However, most of the time, they need to be encouraged a little. So what's the bottom line?

**Here's how to market online:**
1. Know who your people are (your target market).
2. Find the places where they already gather online.
3. Build a presence there.

You've already figured out who your target readers are. So, the next step is to find out where they already gather online. Are there special niche websites or forums for your target readers? Do they read the *Huffington Post* or *Salon.com*? Do they like DIY projects and websites like Instructables.com? Are there print magazines for your topic? Maybe people are gathering at that magazine's website. What email lists do your readers subscribe to? What YouTube channels do they love? All of these questions give you clues as to where your people are gathering. Once you know where they are, all you have to do is establish a presence there.

Maybe building a presence means hanging out on an industry forum. Maybe it means being a guest on a podcast or blog that caters to your target audience. Maybe it means becoming friends with others who serve the same audience. Maybe it means all these things.

As someone once said, it's not about being in the right place at the right time. It's about being in the right place and *staying there*. Use technology and pixels and paid advertising, sure. But understand that the best action you can take is to be present and hang out with people. Your people. The people you want to buy your book and become your clients and customers.

## 5. OFFLINE MARKETING

Second verse, same as the first! To succeed with offline marketing, find where your people gather in "real life" and establish a presence there. Do your people read the local papers or listen to the radio? Put out a press release and try to get journalists to help get the word out about your book. Do your people watch the local news or other TV shows? Send out a segment proposal (similar to a press release, but for television) and see if they'll talk to you on the air. Does your region have a community business organization like a chamber of commerce? See if they'll run a feature about you in their newsletter.

Here are some more ideas to get in front of people offline:

- Hold a launch party at a local art gallery or theater.
- Do book readings at local bookstores, libraries, or schools.
- Organize a regional or national book tour.
- Sponsor a local charity or sports team.
- Write a weekly or monthly column for your local newspaper.
- Ask local businesses whether they'd be interested in selling your book.

There's no end to the possibilities. Just remember, the key is to put your efforts in the places most likely to reach your target audience, not just the largest number of random eyeballs.

## Which Method Works Best?

People are always asking my opinion on the best way to market their book. My answer is always the same. The best marketing strategy is whatever you will do consistently! It doesn't matter if you completely ignore social media, or don't have money for paid advertising, or are too shy to do a podcast or video marketing, or you're too busy to send emails every week. What matters is that you *pick something*—anything, really—and DO IT! Once you get the hang of that strategy, you can add something else. The key is consistency.

I tell people all the time: You can't fail at marketing; you can only fail to **do** your marketing.

This is a long-term process. It takes time for momentum to build up. The biggest mistake authors make is flitting from strategy to strategy, complaining that "none of them work." They won't work if you don't put in the time and effort. It doesn't have to be hard work, it just has to be regular work over time.

A website and email marketing are not negotiable; you need to do those.

Everything else is a choice. Which method will be easy for you? And which one will reach the most people.

## START NOW!

Since it takes time for marketing to build momentum, it's important to start as soon as possible. Like, the minute you decide to write a book, start talking about it. Mention possible titles on your Twitter account. Ask for questions from your current customers. What do they think should be included in your book? Start gathering case studies and success stories from your best clients. This is called engagement—getting others to join you in the process.

When people are engaged in the process, they tend to buy the book and tell everyone they know about it. "Hey, look, I suggested this topic!"

Start marketing like this early on so that, by the time the book is published, the momentum is there. It's incredibly frustrating to put so much time and energy into creating a book, only to find there's no waiting crowd yet. This is a huge mistake authors make. They wait until the book is done to start building buzz. Better late than never, but do yourself a favor and start as soon as possible.

## What is a Platform and How Do You Build One?

If marketing is the act of getting the word out about your book, your platform is where you gather all your people together to talk to them. A blog can be a platform. A podcast or YouTube channel can be a platform. Your email list is definitely a platform. Basically, you need to have a way to talk to people about your book and what you do.

Media is the ultimate platform. In the old days, having your own TV or radio show was the best way to gather any target audience together. Soap operas drew certain types of people together; late night talk shows drew different types of people together.

These older styles of media still work well, but it's difficult to get your own TV show. On the other hand, it's incredibly easy to own online media. Blogs, podcasts, video shows, and social media all offer you a way to quickly and cheaply build your own media platform. You can create your own show in a matter of hours, for very little money.

Podcasts seem to be the most popular form of media right now because people can listen to shows that interest them while they do other things. They can listen while they commute to work, drive the kids to soccer practice, or mow the lawn. It's very difficult to watch a video or read a blog while doing something else.

What do you do once you own your own media platform? You broadcast! Quality and consistency are key here. You want to broadcast information or entertainment (or both) that will attract your target audience. Never forget that they are fickle and can leave just as quickly as they showed up.

Decide on a broadcast schedule that makes sense for

you and your business, then stick to it. Maybe it's a once-a-week blog post. Maybe it's a daily podcast. As long as you're communicating regularly, you're good.

The beauty of having your own media broadcasts is that you have something to tell your email list and social media followers about. People frequently ask me what they should say in their weekly emails and Facebook posts. The answer is to tell people about your most recent episode or blog post. Tease them with it, and get them to click back to your website to see it. Then, go through the episode or post and pull out important points or quotes, slap them on a picture, and you've got Pinterest and Instagram posts.

Start building your platform as soon as possible, if you haven't already. Since your book is about some aspect of your business, creating a platform will not only attract readers, it will attract potential clients and customers. If you start building it early, you'll have an audience of readers ready and waiting by the time your book is published. And, you never know, you might wind up with several new customers before the book is even finished.

## How to Borrow Other People's Platforms

Building your own platform takes time, often a lot of time. So, how can you reach your target audience and gather them to your platform faster? Borrow other people's platforms.

You're looking for places your target readers are already hanging out. If you're a small business advisor, maybe your readers are hanging out on the Forbes blog. Maybe they read

*Entrepreneur* magazine or they listen to the *Entrepreneur on Fire* podcast with John Lee Dumas. Is there a mainstream radio or TV show your people love? Or is there an industry association specifically for your audience? Wherever your target audience gathers in large numbers, you want to be there.

How do you borrow that audience? Offer value to the host or organization. The easiest way to do this is by being a guest—either a guest blogger or an interviewee on a podcast. You could also apply to speak at industry association meetings or conferences. Volunteer to be on the board of directors. Write for the newsletter. Be of service any way you can. Your name and your bio will get out to that audience, usually in the form of "Your name, author of Your Book and host of Your Media." How cool is that?

Make sure you have your own platform set up first, even if there isn't a big audience yet. Demonstrate that you know what you're talking about. Then start making the offers to other media platform owners—don't ask for support, *offer* support.

If you have a podcast or YouTube channel, ask others whether they'd like to be on your show. Offer to interview *them*. Most people will respond positively to your offer of an interview, unless their schedule is so busy that they truly don't have an opening.

After the interview is over, with luck, you've built the beginnings of a strong relationship. Sometimes that person will ask you to be on their show. (Score!) If not, that's okay. Perhaps they'll ask another time. You still have the relationship, which can benefit both of you over the long term.

With guest blog posts, it's even easier. The most popular blogs like the *Huffington Post*, *BuzzFeed*, and *Forbes* survive on their advertising.

They need all the content they can get. The more content they have, the more ads they can show, and the more money they make. So, if you are a good writer, those large blogs can be great exposure for you. Sometimes you have to jump through a few hoops to land a guest spot, but it's worth the extra effort to be seen by their audiences.

Smaller blogs can still be valuable, if their audiences are engaged and read the content week after week. Often, all you have to do to score a guest article with a smaller blog is email the owner with a good pitch. They love having backup content to post when they aren't able to create their own, such as during vacations or when their kids are sick.

Just look around the site for contact information, and shoot them an email. Make it clear you understand their audience, and you want to give them something of value, either information or entertainment. Then pitch them an article that would fit perfectly with the theme and style of the blog.

If they frequently run list articles, pitch a list article. If they run long-form essays, pitch that. And demonstrate how helpful your post would be for their audience. I've pitched hundreds of guest posts over the years, and almost never been turned down, because I think of serving the host's audience first.

## How to Encourage Word of Mouth

The best marketing you'll ever receive is through word of mouth. Get people to talk! One reader tells a friend, and that person tells their boss, and that boss mentions it on Facebook—it goes on and on, if you're lucky.

Smart authors give luck a little help, though. You want to encourage people to talk about your book, without being obnoxious or saying "Spread the word!" too often. Here are a few ways you can encourage word of mouth.

## Create a Sticky Story People Will Remember

A sticky story is one people remember and can easily repeat because it's familiar to them. We all have common childhood experiences and stories to draw from. For example, if you are trying to differentiate your product from two competing products, you might use the story of Goldilocks and the Three Bears.

"This widget is too hot. This widget is too cold. But *this* widget (yours) is just right!" Almost everyone has a common experience with that story. So, it's easy to remember and pass along to others.

Let's say you're a tax accountant and the thing that sets you apart is that you get great results for a lower cost. In this case, you might tell the story like this:

Once upon a time, Goldilocks had to do her taxes. She looked for help from El-Cheapo tax service, but they were too scary (she had heard horror stories about audits).

Then she decided to try Primo Numero Uno, the fancy-pants firm, but they were too expensive!

Finally, she found Your Name Here tax service, and it was just right.

Because we specialize in small business accounting, we can offer fast, reliable service for a much lower price than the fancy-pants firm.

Okay, that was super-simplified. But do you see how setting up a familiar story makes it easy to retell? You can do this with all sorts of cultural references, from *Star Wars* (the scrappy rebels versus the evil empire) to *The Matrix* (the blue pill or the red pill). You can pull from pop culture, history, Hollywood films, sports legends, mythology, childhood stories—anything your target audience will recognize and relate to. Pay special attention to the age range of your target audience. For example, with a *Star Wars* reference, will they relate more to the evil Darth Vader or the cute, precocious Anakin Skywalker?

## Talk About Your Book in Sound Bites

There's a reason the media uses short, snappy taglines to talk about everything. People remember and repeat short and snappy. The most memorable quotes in history are still around because they use the same elements found in sound bites. It can be difficult to think of memorable things to say, until you realize there's a structure involved.

There are elements that make up the structure of a memorable quote. If you want your book and your business to be memorable, try using one or several of these elements in marketing quotes about your book.

**1. Keep it short and to the point.**
"The truth is rarely pure and never simple."
  - **Oscar Wilde**
"Slow but steady wins the race."
  - **Aesop**
"Think globally, act locally."
  - **Paul McCartney**

## 2. Use circular references.

Make a statement, then reverse it. Usually, you'll find two keywords in both parts of the statement, then the words are reversed in the second half of the statement.

"Ask not what your country can do for you; ask what you can do for your country."

-**John F. Kennedy**

"Better a witty fool than a foolish wit."

- **William Shakespeare**

"I meant what I said and I said what I meant."

- **Dr. Seuss**

## 3. Use repetition.

Repeating the same words within one statement helps make it memorable.

"The only thing we have to fear is fear itself."

- **Franklin D. Roosevelt**

"Doubt thou the stars are fire, Doubt that the sun doth move. Doubt truth to be a liar, but never doubt I love."

- **William Shakespeare**

"All you need is love. All you need is love. All you need is love, love… Love is all you need."

- **John Lennon/Paul McCartney**

## 4. Use groups of three.

Our brains are wired to remember three things easily. Because of that, we've also been trained to expect threes to show up in good writing and speeches. Threes appear in the form of descriptions, using three adjectives or adverbs to describe something. You'll also find that a quote can be made up of three separate statements.

"This porridge is too hot. This one is too cold. This one is just right."

**- Goldilocks**

"...government of the people, by the people, for the people, shall not perish from the Earth."

**- Abraham Lincoln**

"The old believe everything, the middle-aged suspect everything, the young know everything."

**- Oscar Wilde**

**5. State something blatantly against common wisdom or knowledge, then explain why it makes sense.**

You can start a quote by stating something that goes against common knowledge or beliefs. This wakes up the brain and makes it pay attention. Then you follow up with another statement about why the first one actually makes sense. The follow-up should make the reader say, "Oh, yeah…I can see that."

"Age is an issue of mind over matter. If you don't mind, it doesn't matter."

**-Mark Twain**

"All our dreams can come true, if we have the courage to pursue them."

**- Walt Disney**

"Giving up smoking is the easiest thing in the world. I know because I've done it thousands of times."

**- Mark Twain**

**6. Use opposites.**

Contrast is one of our most powerful tools as writers. If

you want one thing to stand out, put it in a statement with its opposite.

"The best way to find yourself is to lose yourself in the service of others."

- **Mahatma Gandhi**

"Go to Heaven for the climate, Hell for the company."

- **Mark Twain**

"Did you ever stop to think, and forget to start again?"

- **A. A. Milne**

## 7. Use rhyme and alliteration.

Good quotes and sound bites have a musicality to them. They just roll off the tongue. Often, this is because the author uses rhymes and alliteration as literary devices. Children's books often use these elements to add to the rhythm.

"Today you are you! That is truer than true! There is no one alive who is you-er than you!"

- **Dr. Seuss**

"Promise me you'll always remember: You're braver than you believe, and stronger than you seem, and smarter than you think."

- **A. A. Milne**

"Death is nothing, but to live defeated and inglorious is to die daily."

- **Napoleon Bonaparte**

## 8. Combine elements.

Some of the most memorable quotes in history combine several of these elements. Check it out:

## Chapter Six

"Early to bed and early to rise makes a man healthy, wealthy and wise."
- **Benjamin Franklin**

In this quote, you've got repetition of words (early, early); you've got contrast (early to bed, early to rise); you've got a rhyme scheme (rise, wise); and you've got a group of three (healthy, wealthy, and wise).

"I came, I saw, I conquered."
- **Julius Caesar**

Here we've got repetition (I, I, I) and a group of three.

"You can't fail at marketing. You can only fail to do your marketing."
- **Julie Anne Eason**

Here we've got three sets of repetitions. (you/you, fail/fail, marketing/marketing). And we've got a statement that goes against common wisdom (most people think they can fail at marketing).

"Now this is not the end. It is not even the beginning of the end. But it is, perhaps, the end of the beginning."
- **Winston S. Churchill**

This quote from the famous speech given by Winston Churchill during World War II is a group of three statements. It also contains repetition in groups of three (is/is/is, end/end/end) and circular references (not the beginning of the end, but perhaps the end of the beginning).

Now you know the elements to include, start using them

anytime you're talking or writing about your book or your business. Use them in your speeches, in your web copy, in your sales descriptions—everywhere you can.

The more often you repeat your sound bite, the more often it will be repeated by others. (See what I did there?)

The media, especially, *loves* sound bites. If you can use them in your pitches to TV and radio shows, you'll stand a better chance of getting booked.

It takes practice. One great way to practice is to study famous quotes and pick out the elements. Once you can recognize them in other people's quotes, it's easier to write your own. BrainyQuote.com is a great place to find all sorts of quotes to study.

## Should You Give Away Your Book?

Sometimes you have to prime the pump to get people talking about your book. That means you might need to give away a few (or a lot) of copies. Remember, the goal is not to make money on your book, but rather to get people excited about your business and encourage them to become clients and customers. It's the back end that counts, so getting your book into as many hands as possible is smart.

Be strategic about who you give your book to. Who do they know? How many more people can they reach? Target influencers in your industry, people who have large platforms full of your ideal readers. These might be influential bloggers and podcasters, journalists and TV producers. Or they could be CEOs, association presidents, and event organizers.

If the influencer owns a media channel, like a magazine, blog, or podcast, ask them whether they'd be interested in reviewing your book. If they have influence over employees or vendors, let them know that, if they like the book, you'd be happy to supply copies in bulk at a wholesale discount (40-55% off). Always have a few print copies on hand to give away to potential customers and individuals you meet who might benefit from reading it. You never know who that person knows, or how big an account they might control.

I prefer to give away print copies of my books, simply because people are conditioned to believe that physical books are valuable. They don't get thrown away. However, at $3-$5 a book, that plan can get a little expensive if you're giving away hundreds of copies. It doesn't have to cost a lot of money to give away your books if you offer the ebook version for free, and charge the regular POD price for a print book. Be generous with the influencers, though. Send them a print copy.

## Getting Reviews

We live in a recommendation society now. Before anyone makes a purchase decision, they want to know they're not about to make a mistake. So, they ask their friends, they check comments on blogs, they get opinions on Facebook and Twitter, and they read reviews, especially for books.

Reviews are extremely important, not only to help the reader make a decision whether to buy your book, but also to help your book place better in search engines like Amazon. Which investment book would you choose: one with ten reviews or one with eighty-five? The more reviews you have, the better. It helps if most of them are favorable, but a one-star review every now and then actually lends credibility to the rest of the reviews. We all know no book is going to please *everyone*, so it looks more realistic to have a few bad reviews. Don't freak out when you get those negative ones.

Once you hit around 150-200 reviews on Amazon, its recommendation engine starts taking you more seriously. Your book will probably start showing up higher in search results, and it will be recommended with similar titles more often. So, focus on getting Amazon reviews early and often.

If you're running a best-seller campaign, you definitely want at least five reviews posted on your sales page before the campaign kicks in. So, do a soft launch to your inner circle of friends. Ask them to buy the book on Amazon and leave a review for you. Then, when your campaign kicks off, people will see the reviews and be more likely to purchase the book.

You can also search for top reviewers on Amazon. These are people who frequently review books in your category. Do a little digging to find their contact information, and send them a simple email asking them to review your book. Let them know you've seen their reviews of other books in your category, and you think they'd enjoy your book as well.

### Throw a Party!

Who doesn't love a party? Book celebrations are often thought of as something you do for a launch, like a big kickoff party. However, you can throw a party for your book anytime. Publishing anniversaries are a great excuse for a celebration.

Come up with a theme and a venue that makes sense for your book. People tend to think of business books as dry or stuffy—but not yours! Your book is going to transform lives, and make the world a better place to live. What better reason to celebrate?

Let's say you're a wellness coach and you've written a book on eating healthy, natural ingredients. You might decide to have a book celebration at the local farmer's market or natural living center. If you're a tax accountant, maybe you host an after-hours party for a local business organization like the chamber of commerce. Even if your book is basically a long sales brochure for a piece of machinery you sell, you could still hold a launch celebration at an industry conference or association meeting.

People love happy occasions, and special events like book launches get them talking. If you'd like to learn more about how to host your own book celebration and leverage it for long-term marketing value, there's an entire episode of my podcast devoted to this topic. You can find it at www.SuccessfulAuthorPodcast.com/20.

Remember that book marketing and platform building take time. Lots of time. Put the information in this chapter to work as soon as possible! You might not be able to do everything right away, but you can start building a community on social media. You can start mentioning that you're writing a book. You can get a temporary book cover designed to make it all feel real. And you can start building a mailing list and taking pre-orders for the book. Knowing people are waiting for it will help spur you on when your energy is low and you just don't feel like writing.

Now you know the basics of marketing your book, it's time to look forward. What comes after your book? The profiting stage! What people do *after* they read your book is where the real progress is made.

# CASE STUDY

**Angel Investing:**
**The Gust Guide to Making Money & Having Fun Investing in Startups**
By David S. Rose

**Author's business:** Gust.com (angel investing)
**Target market:** Anyone who is interested in becoming an angel investor, and entrepreneurs who hope to receive funding from such investors

**Tell us about your book.**
Every year in America over 600,000 new businesses start up and hire their first employees. Many will fail, but some of them will become the legendary businesses of the future, transforming industries and making millions for the angel investors who helped fund them in those early days.

Once the exclusive province of multi-millionaire high rollers, angel investing has now entered the mainstream, with more than $20 billion being invested annually by individual investors in the US alone. Contrary to popular belief, access to these high-risk/high-return investments—and success in startup investing —doesn't have to be a matter of luck or connections. *Angel Investing: The Gust Guide to Making Money & Having Fun Investing in Startups* shows how the smart investor with the right strategy and a long-term perspective can achieve annual returns of 25% or more from a well-designed angel portfolio.

## Chapter Six

**How did you find the writing process?**
I printed out several hundred thousand words of answers on the subject that I had written for the website Quora.com. Then I created a table of contents, and worked with a developmental editor to divide the answers according to the topics in the table of contents. Finally, I re-wrote the whole thing into a cohesive book. I enjoy writing and had already drafted much of the book in my Quora answers, so this was relatively easy and fun.

**Did the book help you achieve your goal?**
Our platform is the industry-leading tool set for angel investors, and the goal of the book was to create smart angel investors. Our thought is that anyone who spends more than two seconds looking at the cover of the book is a perfect customer prospect for us. The book was a great success. It hit the New York Times Best Sellers list, was selected as the official training manual for the European Business Angels Network (the EU's pan-regional federation of business angels) and has been purchased in bulk by multiple organizers who have asked me to keynote their conferences.

# Chapter Seven

# Profiting From Your Book

Phew!
You've come a long way, baby. How do you feel?
Exhilarated?
Exhausted?
Hopeful?

Pat yourself on the back. Crack open the champagne. Get yourself a tweed jacket and a pipe. You're a published author!
You've done something that people all over the world are striving for. They'll work and work and most of them will never make it.
But you did.
Well done!

Are you ready for your reward?
All throughout this book I've been telling you that the money comes on the back end. Well, here we are: the back end. It's time to turn those readers into customers.

## How Do You Really Make Money With a Book?

With the old traditional publishing model, authors wrote books and hoped they would sell enough copies to see some royalty income somewhere down the road. Since the publishers put up the money to create the book (paying for editors, cover designers, layout artists, etc.), they received the lion's share of the profits. If a book did really well, an author might be able to make a living.

Unfortunately, the only way for an author to make more money was to go back to the beginning and write another book. And another, and another. Every now and then you got a Malcolm Gladwell or Seth Godin or Stephen King. But in general, counting on royalties is not a great way to make a living.

Fortunately, you already have a business. And your book is going to supplement it nicely. Whatever your topic or industry, creating a back end progression of products and services is how you profit from your book.

If your book is about starting a dog grooming business, for example, you could offer done-for-you business cards and websites. You could brand your own line of pet shampoo or grooming tools. You could create digital information products that walk people through every step of getting their business up and running. And you could create a membership community or industry association to help groomers connect with other people in the business. You could create a high-end one-on-one experience where you set everything up for the new groomer. There's no end to the income streams you could generate from your book topic.

Let's say you own a local bike shop, and you wrote a book on off-road adventures. In addition to the bikes and accessories you already sell at your shop or online, you could lead overnight adventure weekends. You could create videos teaching people how to take care of their bikes. You could sell bicycle accessories online. You could build an app that details the best biking routes in your region. You could set up an after-school biking program for kids. You could move into the camping industry and specialize in biking/camping adventures. Again, your creativity is the only limit for products and services you could create.

It's a good idea to plan out at least some of your back end products and services while you're writing. You'll want to mention them in the book and get people excited about your other offers. At the very least, you'll want to add a page to the back of the book listing them. Start with the products, services, and packages you already have available. Then create new ones that tie into the book.

## Types of Back End Products

There are two types of products you'll want to consider: physical and digital.

**Physical products** are tangible items you can hold in your hand. They can be anything from t-shirts or jewelry to DVDs or automobiles. Anything relevant to your book or your business can be sold as a back end product.

The bike shop owner would naturally tell people he sells bikes and accessories in his store. The dog groomer would tell people about her line of shampoo and brushes. You might already sell these items; you just need to remember to talk about them in the book. Or you may still need to create them. Either way is great.

**Digital products** are usually downloadable or streaming information. PDFs, videos, and audios make up the digital world. They are cheap to make and store online, and they usually don't take a lot of time to create.

Someday we might all have 3-D printers in our homes, and we'll be able to sell digital-to-physical products. Right now, we're limited to downloads.

You might sell a how-to system, a series of recorded interviews, a video course, or a collection of resources. The beauty of digital products is you only have to create them once, and you can sell them over and over again. It doesn't matter whether your audio course gets downloaded one hundred times or ten million times; you only have to create and pay for it once. Pretty sweet!

### Types of Back End Services

Again, you might already have a list of services you offer clients, from business consulting to tax accounting. If so, you can just mention them in your book. However, there may be some creative ways to increase your income by adding extra services. Services can be provided either one-on-one or one-to-many. In other words, you can work with individuals or groups.

Because time is your most valuable resource, one-on-one or done-for-you services should be the most expensive and hardest to qualify for. Those prospects who can't afford to hire you individually might opt for a group program. You can run small or large groups, for a limited time or ongoing for years.

**Membership communities** are a great way to help lots of people (and make lots of revenue) at one time. A typical membership community could have a series of videos offering some core training on a subject, then some limited live interaction with you (through a conference call or Google Hangout), and a forum or Facebook group where members can interact with each other.

**Live events** are another great one-to-many back end service. You can hold one or more events a year where your readers can come and learn more from you and your guests at a live experience. These events might be small workshops or huge conventions, it's up to you. Depending on your industry, you can sell five-figure tickets to very intimate intensive experiences, and wind up making a handsome profit without all the hassle and expense of a big production.

**VIP days** are another great way to serve clients at a very high level, for a short time. It's high-impact consulting. You're there to help the client make a breakthrough in one area as fast as possible. It's like speed-coaching. Many people will pay a premium to get the results they want faster. A full-day or half-day intensive may run into the mid-five figures, depending on the results you're getting for the client. Consultants and coaches can use VIP days once or twice a month, or anytime they need to create more revenue.

Think about the combinations of physical and digital products you can offer that are relevant to your book. Then consider the combinations of relevant one-on-one and group services you can offer. There are no rules here. You can do all of the above, if you want to!

Just because you're a tax accountant doesn't mean you can't sell funny coffee mugs.

## Organize Your Back End Into a Logical Progression

When you go out to eat at a fast food restaurant, what happens? They put everything they have to offer on one big menu; you pick what you want, pay for it, and then take it away in a paper bag. Not exactly a high-end experience, but you get in and out quickly.

When you go to a nice sit-down restaurant, though, what happens there? You are greeted at the door and escorted to a quiet table. The waiter introduces himself and tells you about the specials. Then you have a wine list to look over, and you order drinks. When the waiter comes back, he helps you make a choice between the various appetizers and main courses. After you've enjoyed your meal, he returns again and entices you to order something luscious off the dessert tray—and don't forget the coffee.

When you're selling your back end products and services, you want to be like that waiter at the fine restaurant. Present your offers so they progress in a natural order and slowly escalate in price and value. Once they are well into their customer experience, people can start to choose things that are a little less expensive, too. That's like the coffee and dessert.

To use another metaphor, it's like dating. You're not going to ask someone to marry you on the first date. (At least, I hope you're not.) That special someone needs a little time to get to know you. She needs to go out on a few dates, share a few laughs, and maybe go away for a long weekend. Eventually, she may be ready to meet your parents and settle down with you. But you've got to take each step as it comes.

It's the same with your products. If you offer a $10 book, a $100 video course, a $5000 weekend intensive, and a $50,000 consulting package, where do you start? You start with the lower-priced offers to let people get to know you, then you start moving them up to higher levels of price and value.

Now, there might be some people who read your book and are ready to jump right to your highest level of service. Great! That means you did a good job of earning their trust in the book. Just realize that most folks will need to go through more steps. And many will never reach those higher levels.

The important thing is that you have the steps available for people to take. All too often, authors will design a back end with maybe one small product, or one really expensive consulting package, then they wonder why they have trouble enrolling more people. It's because they don't have enough steps in place. When you're climbing a mountain, you do it in lots of small steps, not one giant step.

Your product progression can be built over time. There's no need to have *everything* in place before you launch your book. However, it's a good idea to have a few offers ready, and then keep adding on over time.

## How to Move People Through Your Product Progression

Once you have a list of products for sale at different price levels, how do you move people along the path? Most importantly, how do you move people from your book to that first product?

Marketers like to talk about sales funnels. These are tools that move people along a path from product to product. Think of a kitchen funnel with a wide top and smaller bottom. Lots of prospects (readers) come in through the wide end of the funnel, a certain percentage of them will buy one low-end product, some of those will buy more products, and a small percentage will purchase your most expensive items. This is a really simplistic image, but you get the point.

One sales funnel might be:
A prospect buys your book.
He joins your mailing list to get a free checklist.
That week, you sell him a $27 video course.
Two months later, you sell him a $500 physical product.
One year later, you sell him a $97-a-month membership.

Another funnel for the same business might be:
A prospect hears you speak at a conference.
She buys your book at the back of the room.
She reads it that evening and asks you some questions the next day.
She signs up for your $10,000 mastermind program.

In those two scenarios, the first prospect might eventually end up in the high-priced mastermind. He just took longer to get there.

You'll naturally have more than one or two sales paths in your business. After all, it's hard to predict every way a prospect might become a customer. However, it's important that you have a few common paths laid out and automated through web pages and emails. Automating the sales process as much as possible gives you the freedom to help your loyal customers and create new experiences for them.

## Chapter Seven

If you don't know already, you'll want to learn how to build automated funnels. However, that's beyond the scope of this book. So, I highly recommend that you read *DotComSecrets* by Russell Brunson if you want to learn how to build an amazing product progression and sell just about anything through a sales funnel.

The profit stage of your book can last as long as you want it to. Depending on your industry, the information might need to be updated now and then. But generally speaking, once you create a product, program, or service, you can keep selling it over and over again.

The key is to keep marketing your book!

Often, authors will spend a few weeks or months getting the word out, and then they just stop.

They move on to something else.

Seriously?

Do you remember how much time and money you spent writing that sucker?

Use it!

Marketing for your book should continue as long as you plan to keep it as part of your funnel. By all means, automate the marketing as much as you can. But don't give up on your book once it's out in the world. The whole reason you invest so much time, energy, and money into publishing a business book is so you have an evergreen sales tool that can be used for years to come.

Don't let your book sit on your desk gathering dust. Sell it. Give it away. Do whatever it takes to get it into the hands of people who need it. People you can serve. People who can become your customers.

## CASE STUDY

**Above & Beyond:**
**How To Help Your Child Get Good Grades In School, and Position Them For Success in College, Career, And Life**
By Dr. Nicoline Ambe

**Author's business:** NicolineAmbe.com (speaker and consultant)
**Target market:** Parents, educators, and parent advocates

**Tell us about your book.**
The book offers parents simple, step-by-step strategies that they can implement at home to help their children improve grades and prepare for a successful future in college and the professional working world.

**Why did you decide to write a book?**
Too many students struggle through school unnecessarily. We live in a competitive global market, and getting a good education and good grades in school is crucial in helping children position themselves for success in this economy. Many parents want to see their children do well in school, but they sometimes lack the resources and tools to help. This book is designed to alleviate their concerns and teach them simple but powerful ideas to help their children excel in their academics. My ultimate goal is to reach as many parents as possible around the world.

**How did you find the writing process?**
I wrote the entire book myself. I paced myself and wrote about

300 words each day. The writing was easy because I did not rush myself; I wrote a little at a time, consistently.

**Did the book help you achieve your goal?**
The results have been outstanding! My book achieved Amazon #1 Best Seller status in two categories and has received over 70 five-star reviews, thanks to the expertise of Best Seller Publishing. Being recognized as a best-selling author has helped improve my book sales tremendously. Business has grown as a result, and I have surpassed my expectations. I have noticed that I sell a lot more books after speaking engagements, and my speaking skills have improved, too. I have also had numerous television appearances on FOX, ABC, NBC and CBS as a result of *Above & Beyond*.

# Conclusion

## What to Expect

It's time to get started.

Are you excited?

I hope so!

Once you start down this book-creation journey, you're going to run into some challenges that I want to prepare you for. Without question, you will experience emotional highs and lows all throughout the project. You'll be zipping along nicely, writing at a good clip, and then BAM! You'll run into what feels like a brick wall. And all sorts of thoughts will swirl around in your head like a cyclone.

*Who am I to write a book?*

*My competitors have more experience.*

*Someone else has already written on this subject; people should just read his book.*

*I'm never going to sell enough copies to make up for the time I'm spending on it.*

*I can't believe how long this is taking.*
*What was I thinking? I flunked English class. I can't even write a grocery list.*
*I have no idea what I'm doing!*

These thoughts are normal, especially in the middle of a project. Self-doubt is common in writers, even when they're normally confident in their everyday lives.

Writing a book can feel like a big risk. After all, what if people don't like it? What if you get bad reviews? What if you don't sell a single copy?

Blah blah blah…

When you catch yourself thinking like this, you need to get out of the negative self-talk whirlwind as quickly as possible.

One way to do that is to ask yourself the opposite questions. What if people *love* it? What if you get rave reviews? What if you sell millions of copies and change the world? (That feels better, doesn't it?)

Another way to get out of your head is to acknowledge the fear, and do it anyway. Thank your brain for trying to take care of you. And let it know that you understand the risks, but you're going to follow through with the plan regardless.

Yet another strategy is to notice patterns around your negative thinking. Is there a certain time of day when you start doubting yourself? Do the voices in your head get louder at the beginning of a new chapter? Or do they pop up when you're hungry or stressed? Once you can recognize a pattern, you can disarm the voices.

For example, my own pattern is feeling nervous at night about whatever project I'm working on. For some reason, the negative voices always show up when I'm done working for the day. It used to be common for me to churn and fret about my writing all night. Then, when I woke up, I'd be full of confidence again.

I learned to recognize the pattern, and now I have a rule—I'm not allowed to listen to any voices in my head after 6 p.m. Period. If I catch myself falling into a negative mindset, I look at the clock. If it's after six, I tell my brain to be quiet. (Funny thing—it's always after six.)

You may have a different pattern and solution. When you catch yourself repeating those negative thoughts, you might need to eat something healthy or go for a walk or call a friend. Having other writers, a mastermind group, or a coach to talk to can help. It's nice to be able to vent to someone who understands what you're going through.

Be careful, though. Choose people who aren't going to enable you and validate your negative self-talk. Choose people who will help you see the patterns, and get you back on track as quickly as possible.

Again, I've never met a writer who didn't have at least a little self-doubt now and then. And that goes for business people, too.

## Procrasti-What?

The next obstacle I want you to be prepared for is stalling techniques. Procrastination is a powerful force. It shows up when you least expect it, and it wears many disguises. It knows exactly how to make you think you're doing something important when, in fact, you're just procrastinating.

Here are just a few creative ways writers put off writing:

- Procrasti-cleaning
- Procrasti-laundry
- Procrasti-drinking
- Procrasti-working
- Procrasti-driving

Seriously, expect that you will find anything to do rather than write when you're in a procrastination mood. Some people will clean out their gutters rather than sit down and write for twenty minutes.

It's not that they don't want to write; it's just resistance showing up. Maybe they don't know what they want to say for the next section they need to write. (Which is why question-based and non-linear writing is so brilliant!) Maybe they're just getting started and fear they'll never finish. Maybe they're nearing the end and have no idea what to do next.

Resistance and procrastination are often rooted in a fear of the unknown. We just don't know exactly how the whole process is going to pan out, so we avoid taking the steps that get us closer to that unknown.

The solution to this is to focus *only* on the next step in front of you. Just that one step. If you made a commitment to write for an hour a day, do that. Don't think about the next stage until the current stage is done. Don't worry about finding an editor until you're done writing. Don't worry about publishing until you're done with a draft. You can research a little bit, or ask around for referrals, just don't let it stop you from doing the work you need to do right now.

How do you know what you need to do right now? Break each stage down into ridiculously tiny chunks and ask questions. Remember, your brain is wired to answer questions. So, a question will always get your brain working on an answer. If you follow the planning stage and create a question-based outline, you will never be without a question to answer in the manuscript.

But what about all the other things you need to do? Once you're finished writing, then what? Fear of *that* unknown can sometimes stop you from moving forward, too. If you know the editing stage comes next, write out a list of questions that will pull you forward through that stage. Instead of telling yourself, "I need to find an editor." ask smaller questions, such as:

- Who can I ask for editor referrals?
- What sample piece shall I ask potential editors to review before I hire them?
- How much am I willing to pay for an editor?
- Do I want to use a structural editor? Or go straight to copyediting?
- Who will I use for beta readers?
- What do I need to include in the style guide I give to an editor?
- What timeline do I need my editor to follow?

Do you see how breaking the steps down into smaller questions helps you find the next action you need to take?

If you answered the editing referrals question with "Bob, Larry, and Sarah", then your next step would be to contact those people and see if they know any good editors. If you answered the sample piece question with "Chapter Seven", then your next step is to pull out Chapter Seven and prepare to send it to your potential editors. Answer the questions, and the next steps will appear. It's magic.

Expect that you will run into resistance, procrastination, and the unknown. Be prepared for all of these, and don't let anything stop you from moving forward!

## Be Fearless!

So much procrastination happens in the name of fear.

If you're procrastinating, and you think fear may be behind it, ask yourself: what's the worst that could happen?

People don't buy your book?

People don't like your book?

Boo-hoo . . . move on!

Your book is not the only thing you're ever going to do in your life.

Your book is *not* you.

Your book is a tool. It's a business tool, just like your website.

Do you fret and worry over whether people will like your website? Maybe a little, but its success isn't based on whether people "like" it. Success is defined by how well it works.

Go back to your planning document. What is the goal for your book? To bring in customers? To inspire? To entertain? To inform?

Did it do that?

Then it's a success!

## Chapter Seven

So many people come to me and say they're having problems finishing (or starting) their books. I've discovered the root problem is almost always fear. They're afraid of looking foolish. They're afraid of what others will think. They're afraid of the unknown.

Here's the deal. Six months after you publish your book, one of three things could happen.

A. Your book could completely bomb, and you'll have moved on to another project.
B. Your book could be a raging success, and you'll be enjoying the growth of your business.
C. Your book could be a modest success, and you'll be working to promote it to more people.

Let's get a little perspective here. You're not going to *die* if your book bombs. You'll just move on to something else.

But what if that book truly helps just a handful of people? Wouldn't that be worth it? What if one—just one person—loves your book so much that they refer you to all their friends, and your business takes off? Wouldn't that be worth it?

The truth is, you have absolutely no idea how many people you might impact with your book—or how deeply you may affect the world as a whole. Authors start ripples, and often they have no idea how important those ripples will turn out to be in one year, or ten, or a hundred.

So what are you waiting for? Get it done!

Stop putting it off and letting the "What Ifs" keep you stuck. You can absolutely do this!

## Immediate Action Steps

Don't wait another minute to get started on this journey. You know the basic process now.

You don't need to learn any more about it; you need to start. So, here are the first steps to take.

**1. Download the planning workbook.** Even if you've already started writing your book, do yourself a favor and go through the planning exercises. They will help you move forward through the writing process and the publishing and marketing phases faster.

**2. Set up your platform.** Yes, do it before you even start writing. If you wait until you're done with your book, it will be much harder to gain momentum in the marketing phase. Dig your well before you're thirsty.

**3. Write your book.** Make a commitment and stick with it. You know what to expect with the emotional ups and downs. You'll be on the lookout for those sneaky procrastination techniques. Just sit your butt down and write. The first draft is supposed to be a mess, so don't worry about making it perfect.

**4. Get some support during the process.** I don't want to overwhelm you with too many action steps. You've read this far, so you already know what comes next. If you'd like some support along the way, consider joining a community of people who can guide you along the path. Maybe that means a local writing group, or maybe it means getting assistance from start to finish by joining my Nonfiction Book Academy. I'd love to welcome you to our community of authors.

## Chapter Seven

You know what?
You got this.
The world is waiting for your book!

P.S. Please stay in touch and let me know when your book is published. I want to be the first to congratulate you on your major accomplishment.

I also want to help you tell the world!

Email me at:

IdidIt@NonfictionBookAcademy.com

# YOU'RE INVITED!

It's time you finished your book and got your message out into the world in a big way. Now that you know the process, there's nothing standing in your way.

Except maybe procrastination.

And doubt.

And isolation.

I don't want *anything* to stop you from publishing your book. So, I've created a special community where you can get my personal support and guidance with writing your book, getting published, and reaping the benefits of becoming an author.

It's called the Nonfiction Book Academy, and this is your invitation to come check out the growing list of CEOs, speakers, coaches, consultants, service providers, retailers, non-profits, and other business people who are finally becoming authors.

**Find out more at www.NonfictionBookAcademy.com**

# CASE STUDY

**Plans to Prosper:**
**Strategies, Systems & Tools for Small Business Marketing Success**
By Victoria Cook and Stan Washington

**Authors' business:** Center For Guilt Free Success (Marketing consulting)
Target market: Micro and small business owners

**Tell us about your book.**
*Plans to Prosper: Strategies, Systems & Tools for Small Business Marketing Success* is a step-by-step guide to growing businesses through effective marketing. We take the guesswork out of marketing strategies in order to help save you money. In this book, you will learn how to

- Choose a marketing strategy that's right for you.
- Market in a short period of time on a small budget while increasing visibility, raising buyer awareness, and growing sales.
- Profit from the marketing mistakes other small business owners have made and avoid making the same mistakes.

We also provide examples, tips, resources, and warnings to help guide your business toward focused growth.

**How did you find the writing process?**
Stan and I wrote the book together. We formulated the outline

and divided up the writing. We began in mid-August, and completed it in December. We met virtually weekly for a couple hours to review progress, make changes, and work on the book structure. We did have a professional editor edit the book.

**Did the book help you achieve your goal?**
Our goal was to position ourselves as experts, elevate our credibility, gain larger and more paid speaking opportunities, and provide small business owners with resources for marketing effectively. The results have been great so far. I have already had back-of-the-room sales at the two small speaking engagements so far this year. Sales are converting at 16% of the room.

## CASE STUDY

**The Nehemiah Effect:**
**Ancient Wisdom from the World's First Agile Projects**
By Ted Kallman and Andrew Kallman

**Authors' business:** PMObrothers.com (consulting and speaking on agile methodology)
**Target market:** Project managers, consultants, and executives who want to use agile methods

**Tell us about your book.**
*The Nehemiah Effect* combines new mindsets, methodologies, and technologies with proven, ancient wisdom to deliver surprising results for today's business leaders and project managers. The book is a deconstruction of The Book of Nehemiah, showing how agile practices were used 2,500 years ago to successfully deliver a huge project with 50,000 volunteers. In other words, while agile methods are considered new and innovative, they were actually used centuries ago.

**Why did you decide to write a book?**
We wrote the book to position ourselves as thought leaders in our industry and to market our consulting and speaking practices both in Europe and the US.

**How did you find the writing process?**
We co-wrote the book, which took roughly two years. The process was not easy since we were both working full-time and living in different countries.

**Did the book help you achieve your goal?**

We first used social media to market the book, individually reaching out to over 5,000 people in our combined networks. The book became an Amazon #1 best-seller through these efforts. We then worked with Rob Kosberg and his team at Best Seller Publishing to keep the momentum going. To date the book has over 50 five-star reviews and has become a #1 best-seller for four out of the last 14 months, #2 on the best-seller list for another three months and has been featured in the top 10 every other month.

Our speaking engagements over the last 12 months have increased tremendously, and our speaking fees have also increased. We have new clients consistently tracking us down because of the book. We were already confident that we had a good and valuable product, but the book really positioned us as the experts in the industry.

We are now working with high profile clients like General Motors and Whirlpool, who might never have heard of us if they didn't have the book in hand. We are currently working on co-authoring a second book, *Flow: Beyond Agile*.

# CASE STUDY

**Access Granted:**
**A retired Special Agent's insider look into obtaining your government security clearance fast and efficiently, overcoming background issues, and exploding your career and income in the process.**
By Kevin A. Crane

**Author's business:** Ameri-Sec Background & Clearance Corporation (security clearance consulting)
**Target market:** College students and people who need security clearance

**Tell us about your book.**
The book provides detailed, yet easy-to-understand explanations, strategies, tips, and guidance on how to obtain a federal government security clearance quickly and efficiently, based on my 21 years of experience conducting and supervising these types of investigations.

**Why did you decide to write a book? What was the ultimate goal?**
For ten years, I yearned to write a book in order to leave a positive legacy and help others with the information I had stored in my head. My ultimate goal was to use the book as a platform leading to paid speaking engagements for college students looking to prepare themselves for post-graduation careers. I knew the information in my book could be used to not only help students obtain a government security clearance, but

also to prepare them for a background investigation required as a prerequisite for any job.

**How did you find the writing process?**
I wrote the book myself in about three months. The type of information I wanted to provide really needed to come from me, so the readers could easily comprehend it. I would definitely say it was more challenging than I thought. It would have been easy to just not write the book at all. It was absolutely worth the brief struggle to achieve a book that I was proud of!

**Did the book help you achieve your goal?**
I am thankful to have found Best Seller Publishing to help me reach my goal. Within about a week of releasing the book, I became a # 1 best-selling author in four different categories on Amazon.com! I did achieve my original goal of not only writing a book, but writing a book that could help so many people.

As a result of my book, I've been featured in news articles, have spoken on numerous radio shows, and have been interviewed on live television shows including Fox News and NBC. I have interviews set for ABC, CBS, and another Fox News show. Becoming an author has provided me with personal and professional fulfillment, and opportunities that never would have entered my life otherwise. It has practically guaranteed me excellent teaching and earning opportunities. Had I not written my book, I would always have lived with regret…that will never happen now!

# Acknowlegements

Writing a book truly takes a village. I am forever grateful to all the people who helped make this book a reality.

Especially...

James: You are my everything.

Catey, Sarah, and Ben: Thank you for being independent, cooking your own meals, and understanding how much time and energy it takes to write a book.

Catherine Neuhardt-Minor: Thank you for always believing in me, even when you thought I was crazy.

Tracey Charlebois: Thanks for being my partner in crime and conspirator in all things awesome!

Julia Willson: Thanks for your wonderful editing and for showing up exactly when I needed you.

Julie Salisbury and the team at Influence Publishing: Thanks for all you've done to make this a better book.

Dave Jabas: Thank you for all your support and attention.

Damian Boudreaux: Thank you for showing me how to be who I AM.

Benji Rabhan: Thank you for teaching me the power of perseverance (especially when writing a book).

# Author Biography

Julie Anne Eason has been a professional writer for over 20 years. After figuring out that fiction writing wasn't for her, she turned to freelance journalism and copywriting for a living in order to stay home and raise her three children. As technology advanced, she witnessed the balance of power in the publishing industry shift. Once the big New York publishers held all the cards. Writers were "lucky" if they could land an agent or a book contract. But now individuals are taking the initiative and writing, publishing, and marketing their own books without the need for an agent or publisher to give them a chance — which means that *finally* businesses, non-profits, and entrepreneurs can take advantage of the amazing power of books to spread their messages and promote their products.

Today she ghostwrites books for entrepreneurs, speakers, coaches, CEOs, and other business people who want to expand their reach and build their brands. She has combined her love for marketing and writing to create *The Successful Author Podcast*, where she interviews book industry experts on writing, publishing, and marketing books.

Since she can only ghostwrite a few books each year, she has dedicated herself to empowering others to write their own books by creating the Nonfiction Book Academy. This is an online mentoring program where authors and soon-to-be authors can get the caring support and guidance they need to finally write, publish, market, and profit from their books.

You can find out more at www.NonFictionBookAcademy.com

# About the Author

You can find Julie hanging out in the following locations:

**WEBSITES:**
www.JulieAnneEason.com
www.TheProfitableBusinessAuthor.com
www.NonfictionBookAcademy.com

**PODCAST:**
www.SuccessfulAuthorPodcast.com

**SOCIAL MEDIA:**
Facebook: https://www.facebook.com/julieAeason
Twitter: @BizBookWriter
Instagram: SuccessfulAuthorPodcast

**WANT HELP GETTING YOUR BOOK FINISHED?**
Join our Writing Accountability Group on Facebook
www.facebook.com/groups/writingaccountability

Take the Reach Out and Write Challenge to finish your book in one year.
www.ReachOutandWrite.com

Get daily text messages to inspire and remind you to *Keep Writing*.
In the US or Canada: Text @writee to 81010
Internationally: Download the *Remind* app on your mobile device, and join the class writee.

CPSIA information can be obtained at www.ICGtesting.com
Printed in the USA
BVOW06s1223050915

415977BV00003B/3/P